The Word I'm Thinking Of

A DEVILISH DIC )S

Michael Gates

ZABRISKIE STREET PRESS

ISBN: 0-615-73818-4
ISBN-13: 978-0-615-73818-5

For my family

CONTENTS

INTRODUCTION

I love words. It's strange the byways of memory that stumbling across a certain word or phrase will take you down, especially if it's one you're discovering and finding the meaning of for the first time. This book records some of the reveries that unusual words have elicited in me.

From an early age, I've been an avid reader of literature and interested in expanding my vocabulary. In high school, I received a score of over 700 on my SAT verbal test, and so decided I should pursue a career that somehow involved working with words. In my work as a professional copyeditor, that's what I do, though I rarely encounter words as unusual as those collected here. So I've set out to enhance my vocabulary on my own. It's an ongoing, lifelong project.

Most of the words you'll find here were originally defined and commented on in my spare-time avocation as a blogger (at michaelgates.blogspot.com). I've been collecting rare words for more than ten years now and only recently thought of collecting them in book form. I hope you'll find them as fascinating and thought-provoking as I do.

Where did I find these curious and difficult words, you may well ask. Sometimes it was by stumbling across them while reading. Often though, I deliberately sought them out online. A Google search for "weird" or "unusual" (or even "useless") words will reveal many websites devoted to collecting rare lexemes.

For each word highlighted here, I've included a quotation to show how the word can be used in context. These quotations sometimes come from my own reading, but more often from searching Google Books or some other online source for a (public domain) literary quotation containing the word. All of these quotes are attributed to the original authors when that can be determined. "Quotations" and commentaries that aren't attributed to someone else are attributable to me!

I haven't included many etymologies in this book, as that information can be fairly easily found in more conventional dictionaries and online. My hope is that this book will help to revive interest in some of these words. Please do try to use them in your daily conversations. Think of it as a humorous social-science experiment to see what kinds of reactions you receive. For example, you might say "That was a very interesting flumadiddle you raised at the meeting today." Or: "I like that flumadiddle you're wearing! Where did you get it?" And please report back to me any blank look, inquiry as to your meaning, or sincere "thank you" you record. I'm easy to find online.

Michael Gates
Jersey City, New Jersey
April 2013

A

aboulomania [ay-BOO-lo-MAY-nee-a] (noun)

Pathological indecisiveness

"Chocolate or strawberry? Cursing his **aboulomania**, Sylvester continued to stare at the ice-cream parlor's menu."

absquatulate [ab-SQOTCH-uh-layt] (verb)

To leave in a hurry; vamoose

"'Time to **absquatulate**,' Hiram whispered to himself as the drapes went up in flames."

I was playing with a three-legged cat one night at a friend's house. I offered kitty a catnip toy, but it seemed to startle him. He **absquatulated**. I was a little miffed, but then he came back and sniffed it. Nice kitty. It's amazing how fast a three-legged cat can move.

abstemious [ab-STEE-mee-us] (adjective)

Restraint in consuming food or alcohol

"'I'm pretty **abstemious** myself,' Ralph explained. 'Partly because there have been some family issues with alcohol—but I've been known to take a drink after a hard day in the salt mine.'"

abulia [uh-BOO-lee-uh] (noun)

A symptom of a mental disorder involving inability to make decisions or a loss of volition

"When **abulia** increases with her—in consequence of fatigue, for instance—insomnia increases also at the very time when she should know how to sleep."

—Pierre Janet, *The Mental State of Hystericals* (1901)

I can't decide what I want to say about **abulia**. Actually, I can: I think it's a pretty common affliction. I know I dither over, for example, whether to buy raspberry or blackberry jam at the supermarket. First-world problems!

I recall that I was once watching an excellent production of *Hamlet* on PBS, a play that is *all about* **abulia** ("To be or not to be..."), and couldn't decide whether to switch channels to watch the premiere of a new TV series called *Happy Town*. I can't decide if I should tell you what I decided—which probably tells you something.

accismus [ak-SISS-muss] (noun)

Pretending not to be interested in something while secretly being interested in it

"**Accismus** is sometimes considered as a virtue, sometimes as a vice, which Augustus and Tiberius practiced with great success. Cromwell's refusal of the crown of England may be brought as an instance of an **accismus**."
—*The New and Complete American Encyclopedia* (1805)

This is what is called "being coy." Julius Caesar refuses the crown, even though he desires it, knowing that the people will insist all the harder that he accept it. The fox pretends he really doesn't like grapes.

If you're interested in something—or someone—but try to hide it, for whatever reason, you're engaging in **accismus**. Just pretend you've never heard of this word.

acephalia [ace-uh-FAYL-ya] (noun) **acephalic** (adjective)

The absence of a head or the absence of a brain

"Comparative anatomy, and **acephalic** monstrosities among the mammalia and man, furnish incontrovertible proofs of the brain not being the origin of the nervous system at large."
—Johann Gaspar Spurzheim, *The Anatomy of the Brain* (1826)

Yoko Ono once said, "Consider if it is such a catastrophe to live without your head." She added that it might make it easier to move around, since one's body would be so much lighter. Zen humor aside, I can't imagine what it would be like to live in a state of **acephalia**. I often live in my head—the curse or blessing of the introvert, depending on how you look at it. I do have a rich interior life that would be hard to give up.

I wouldn't mind getting rid of the nattering jukebox of stuck records that is sometimes set to forte in my head, though.

ackamarackus [AK-uh-muh-RAK-uss] (noun)

Nonsense, especially if pretentious; something deceptive; humbug
"Aunt Betty was quite an amusing conversationalist and enjoyed sending us witty postcards filled with charming non-sequiturs, ackamarackus, and bon mots."

Of course, I would never engage in such balderdash except when I have to conduct personal business that involves writing to some bureaucratic entity—then I turn on the **ackamarackus** faucet. I start my email with a salutation like "Dear [blank] Officer" (no matter how lowly the recipient) and then compose my request or inquiry using the diction and sentence structure of a honey-tongued aristocrat: "may I inquire," "would it be acceptable," "could I be so bold as to," "naturally you may wonder," "perhaps you would consider," etc. They seem to lap it up.

adoxography [ad-ox-OG-ruh-fee] (noun)

Skilled writing on a trivial subject

"He discards the tricks of the school, **adoxography**, epigram, and, as a rule, paradox. Simplicity is his charm."
—T. R. Glover, *The Conflict of Religions in the Early Roman Empire* (1909)

Maybe "**adoxography**" would be a good name for a book such as this....
I first encountered this word in a book about fish, of all things, so let me attempt some fishy **adoxography** here. A company in Taiwan has developed a tropical fish that glows in the dark. It's a zebra fish (one of the most common aquarium critters—I own four non-glowers) that's been

genetically modified with jellyfish DNA to give off a ghostly green light. It's also been made sterile, so it won't breed more eerie glowfish if it somehow gets loose in lakes and rivers. It might make an odd but fun addition to an aquarium, though they're rather pricey at $17 per. I find that my pet fish die too often to flush 17 bucks down the toilet every time one expires.

If we have to play God with DNA, I suppose glowing is a benign enough innovation. What's alarming, though, is that other companies are apparently working on modified fish from the tropics that will survive at colder temperatures. And that could present a big problem, even if they're sterile. Just imagine dipping your foot into your favorite lake or stream and having it nibbled on by a piranha. Skilled writing on that topic would not be **adoxography.**

affictitious [af-ik-TISH-us] (adjective)

Meaning feigned; counterfeit

"The forger was caught despite his masterfully crafted **affictitious** signatures."

afflatus [uh-FLEY-tuss] (noun)

An inspiration, a creative impulse

"Walter's window faced a brick wall, so, seized by a sudden **afflatus**, he leaned out and painted a landscape on it."

"She did not think herself a genius by any means; but when the writing fit came on, she gave herself up to it with entire abandon....The divine **afflatus** usually lasted a week or two, and then she emerged from her 'vortex,' hungry, sleepy, cross, or despondent."
—Louisa May Alcott, *Little Women* (1869)

If you have an **afflatus**, write it down! (Carry a notebook.) They tend to evaporate quickly, in my experience. (The **afflatus**, not the notebooks.)

alible [AL-uh-bull] (adjective)

Having nutrients; nourishing

"'I care not how **alible** it is,' Humphrey hissed as he tossed his Christmas gift, a colorful fruitcake, out of the window."

There. A perfectly **alible** use of an obscure word, that. I feel more intelligent just knowing what it means.

ambry [AM-bree] (noun)

A storeroom or cupboard; pantry; closet

"'Stuff it in your **ambry**,' she advised. Karl felt mystified and vaguely insulted."

ampullosity [am-pul-OSS-ih-tee] (noun)

Pretentious inanity or bombast

"'Call it **ampullosity**,' said Jessica, 'but I am full of fractals of renewed delight this evening.'"

amyloid [AM-uh-loyd] (adjective)

Containing or relating to starch; starchy

"'These shirts are too **amyloid**!' exclaimed Dr. Klaxon. The laundry staff looked mystified."

anastrophe [uh-NASS-truh-fee] (noun)

Inversion of the normal syntactic order of words

"Elided prepositions suffer **anastrophe** only when they as adverbs modify a verb to be supplied."
—Bernadotte Perrin and Thomas Day Seymour, *Eight Books of Homer's Odyssey* (1897)

Thanks to my *Star Wars*-obsessed offspring, I'm aware that the most famous **anastropher** in contemporary popular culture is Yoda, who talks like this:

"To my *Star Wars*-obsessed offspring, thanks. Aware I am that the most famous **anastropher** in contemporary culture Yoda is…."

anfractuous [an-FRAK-choo-us] (adjective)

Full of twists and turns, winding, tortuous

"Miguel's **anfractuous** blathering is driving me barmy."

"**Anfractuous**." That could be alternate name for my blog, which is about nothing more than the meanderings of my mind.

anfractuosity [an-frak-choo-OS-ity] (noun)

The quality of having many twists and turns

"There are chance **anfractuosities** of ruin in the upper portions of the Coliseum which offer a very fair imitation of the rugged face of an Alpine cliff."
—Henry James, *Italian Hours* (1909)

Speaking of Henry James, he's a pretty **anfractuous** writer, in my reading experience. Even the title of perhaps his most famous work, *The Turn of the Screw*, is twisty. And here's a typically anfractuous Jamesian sentence: "He fairly caught himself shooting rueful glances, shy looks of pursuit, toward the embodied influence, the definite adversary, who had, by a stroke of her own, failed him, and on a fond theory of whose palpable presence he had, under Mrs. Newsome's inspiration, altogether proceeded." If you can parse that, you're a better ex-English major than I am.

animadvert [an-uh-mad-VERT] (verb)

To remark or comment critically, usually with censure or strong disapproval; used with "on" or "upon"

"'If you are going to **animadvert** upon my nose ring, Mother,' said Mariellen, 'allow me to critique your collagen injections.'"

anodyne [AN-uh-dine] (noun or adjective)

Something that lessens pain; something that isn't likely to disturb or annoy

"Now, the **anodyne** had not produced the effect which it appeared to have done; instead of healthful sleep, it had brought on a kind of light-headed somnolence, in which the mind, preternaturally restless, wandered about its accustomed haunts, waking up its old familiar instincts and inclinations."
—Edward Bulwer-Lytton, *Zannoni* (1842)

One night, as part of a local celebration, I stopped by an art gallery on Jersey Avenue. (In Jersey City in New Jersey—everything was "Jersey" that night. I should have worn a jersey.) The "show" there included a display of living plants, dead mice and a dissected rat in various containers, along with a variety of tablets and pills (and dirt for the plants). It seemed to be an aesthetic and quasi-scientific examination of the effect of, say, Tylenol (**anodyne**!) or penicillin on philodendrons, rodent flesh, and such. Not an **anodyne** experience, but one I won't soon forget.

antimacassar [anti-ma-CASS-ar] (noun)

An embroidered, doily-like cover to protect the back or arms of furniture

"But the small room within was empty, in John's eyes, although, indeed, Eliza Jennings sat in a big chair, with a crocheted **antimacassar** on its back, rocking comfortably."
—Margaret Deland, "Sidney," in *The Atlantic Monthly* (1890)

I remember my grandmother's stuffed chairs having **antimacassars**, though I didn't know what they were called back then. I always thought they were just for decoration, but it seems they served a purpose back when men oiled their hair with an oil called Macassar. Without them, the greasy stuff would stain the furniture when they leaned back against the upholstery—to light their pipes no doubt.

antipodean [an-tip-uh-DEE-un] (adjective)

Opposite to or of another thing

"Then, indeed, does the tuckered sylph come out in fairy form and proceed

15

with joy under cousinly escort to the exhausted old assembly-room, fourteen heavy miles off, which, during three hundred and sixty-four days and nights of every ordinary year, is a kind of **antipodean** lumber-room full of old chairs and tables upside down."
—Charles Dickens, *Bleak House* (1853)

I love Dickens, but he wrote as if he was being paid by the word. Maybe he was. **Antipodean** of, say, Hemingway.

antithalian [anti-THAY-li-an] (adjective)

Opposed to fun

"Mr. Toobad described her as being fully impressed with the truth of his Ahrimanic philosophy, and being altogether as gloomy and **antithalian** a young lady as Mr. Glowry himself could desire for the future mistress of Nightmare Abbey."
—Thomas Love Peacock, *Nightmare Abbey* (1818)

"Ahrimanic" refers to Ahriman, which in Zoroastrianism is the name for a devil or Satan. Would you describe Satan as **antithalian**? It depends on what kind of fun you're into, I guess.

arsiversie [AR-see-VAR-see] (adjective)

Meaning upside down (?)

"[H]e was a botcher, cheese-eater, and trimmer of man's flesh embalmed, which in the **arsiversie** swagfall tumble was not found true."
—François Rabelais, *Gargantua and Pantagruel* (1567)

I *think* this word means "upside down." It's hard to find a definition for it.
    I've always enjoyed looking at the topsy-turvy sky and world you can see on the surface of a calm lake. One dropped pebble and the universe is destroyed in a burst of concentric circles. It gives you a new perspective on things. Maybe I should spend more time **arsiversie**.

asseverate [uh-SEV-er-ate] (verb)

To declare earnestly or solemnly; affirm positively

"Paul's three-year-old would frequently **asseverate** any recent use of the 'potty.'"

astonied [uh-STAHN-eed] (adjective)

Being in a bewildered state; dazed

"Pavel had never been on a roller coaster before, and he exited the Scream Machine looking **astonied**."

ataraxia [at-uh-RAK-see-uh] (noun)

Peace of mind; emotional tranquility

"Alastair found **ataraxia** in a rocking chair."

atrabilious [at-ruh-BIL-yuss] (adjective)

1. Gloomy; melancholic
2. Irritable; peevish

"Serena refused to invite the **atrabilious** Mr. Morne, who could spoil a party just by opening his mouth."

autoschediastic [auto-skee-dee-AS-tic] (adjective)

Extemporaneous or improvised

"In concluding, the Editors would remark, that all the criticisms in their work are to be considered as '**autoschediastic**' (a much nicer word than extemporaneous, or off-hand), because, as soon as they are finished, they are dispatched to the press, and that very little opportunity is afforded to them of correcting those errors, and supplying those defects, which a leisurely and careful revision could not fail to discover."
—*The Quarterly Review* (London) (1820)

Here's something I wrote in my blog one day in a moment of

autoschediastic mania:

"While standing in line at the bank today, I saw a woman wearing a (faux) leopard-skin hat. It reminded me of Bob Dylan's song, 'Leopard-Skin Pillbox Hat,' on the album *Blonde on Blonde*. When I think of a blonde (with an 'e' on the end), I think of Marilyn Monroe, who sang 'Diamonds Are a Girl's Best Friend' in one of her films and, speaking of diamonds, was married to a baseball player, Joe DiMaggio. DiMaggio, after his baseball career ended, became a TV pitchman for Mr. Coffee, a machine for making . . . coffee. And I love coffee. I like to grind the beans myself, and drink it black. 'Black as midnight on a moonless night,' as FBI agent Dale Cooper said when asked how he liked his coffee. Cooper was a character on a TV show, one of my all-time favorites, called *Twin Peaks*. The peaks referred to in the show's title were two mountains, although the phrase 'twin peaks' is supposedly also a juvenile euphemism, referring to a woman's breasts. There are many euphemisms for parts of the body, both male and female, most of them 'vulgar slang,' as the dictionary says. One of them is 'pussy.' A pussy is also a cat, a feline, and leopards are members of the cat family. Before leopards became endangered, their spotted skin was highly prized for use in women's coats and, at one time, 'pillbox'-style hats."

B

banjax [BAN-jaks] (verb or noun)

To break or smash; also: a mess

"'It's kind of scary,' Ethan said. 'If one of those strands of DNA was **banjaxed** or configured in a different way, I might be a different person—an albino hermaphrodite, perhaps, or a seven-foot elephant man.'"

I'm tired of seeing **banjaxed** old pre-digital TV sets on the curbside, their cathode-ray tubes exposed and their circuit wires hanging out like the disemboweled intestines of some slaughtered creature. Don't people know that you can't just throw away a TV set? The sanitation department will not pick them up, since they're considered hazmat with all the poisonous chemicals used in their manufacture. You have to take them somewhere, like the Incinerator Authority (in our fair city) or whatever the equivalent place is that accepts old appliances, paint and aerosol cans, and dead batteries. Then they perhaps get shipped off to a Chinese landfill. But at least we wouldn't have to look at these sad, **banjaxed** relics of a bygone era and stumble over them for weeks on end while their ignorant owners wait for a trash pick-up that will never come.

barmecidal [bar-muh-SIGH-dul] (adjective)

Presenting only the illusion of abundance

"Zenobia had a vast collection of wax and plastic fruit, which she called her **barmecidal** feast."

battologize [buh-TOL-uh-jize] (verb)

To repeat oneself excessively

"But when we pray, let us not **battologize** (i.e., use vain repetitions), but theologize."

—Samuel Miller (quoting the early Christian theologian Origen), *Thoughts on Public Prayer* (1849)

It can be annoying when someone keeps repeating himself, but it can be amusing, too. Whenever you hear the word or catchphrase elsewhere, you think of that person. The verbal tic becomes symbolic of him or her, like a sonic monogram or an aural coat of arms.

As the Beatles said, *Yeah, yeah, yeah.*

Here are some words and phrases I hear from **battologizers** (who shall be nameless) all the time:

circle back
close the loop
have a conversation about....
pretty much
exactly!
What's interesting is....
Can I ask you a question?
over to you
okay, okay, okay
Here's the thing...
whatcha got?

benthos [BEN-thoss] (noun)

The biogeographic region that includes the bottom of an ocean, lake, or sea, and littoral and supralittoral shore zones

"Everywhere on the foreshore except in the most desolate of localities the **benthos** provides a living, scanty though it may be, for inshore fishermen."
—James Johnstone, *Conditions of Life in the Sea* (1908)

I clean my aquarium periodically, as its **benthos**(as I call it) gets a bit grubby. This always brings on thoughts of the ocean and the beach and summer approaching—and an old poem I wrote:

Beach Day

It resembles a limeade spritz:
this crashing of the sea.

The rock pool pumps
like a heart.

Foam suggests
mounds of dirty meringue

or nothing in particular.
I've run out of metaphors.

Up on the highway,
a rumble machine

wavers in the heat and rolls
its belt of black tar.

Stones will be sand
one of these millennia.

I lie down, thinking of magma
spreading its ooze of fire,

and the whole day dissolves.
They will find me fossilized

like a Mesozoic fish
in a stone that falls out of a wall.

[The End... **benthos** or bathos?]

bizarrerie [biz-ar-er-EE] (noun)

Something bizarre

"It was a freak of fancy in my friend to be enamored of the Night for her own sake; and into this **bizarrerie**, as into all his others, I quietly fell; giving myself up to his wild whims with a perfect abandon."
—Edgar Allan Poe, "The Murders in the Rue Morgue" (1841)

My wife recently returned to our abode with an item she found in someone's trash receptacle on a nearby byway: a bone-white mannequin's arm, which has now joined the collection of imitation, alabaster body parts we keep in an antiquarian wheelchair in a corner of our living room. Do we live in a **bizarrerie**? Some might think so. But most visitors seem to find it both funny and... funny. Judge for yourself—by appointment only.

blatherskite [BLATH-er-skite] (noun)

1. A babbling, foolish person
2. Absurd and foolish talk

"'Oh, that's nothing but **blatherskite**!' cried Miranda when Viola suggested that Mr. Crave might only be interested in her fortune."

blatteroon [blat-er-OON] (noun)

Someone who boasts or babbles senselessly; someone who won't shut up

"And military circles throughout the length and breadth of the land are torn up because of a tiff between a pompous old **blatteroon** and a noisy boy, caused by a suit of clothes! Uncle Sam should detail a nursery maid of vivandiere to lay Johnny across a vinegar barrel and beat the reveille on his basement with a clapboard, and send McCook to some well-regulated lunatic asylum."
—William Cowper Brann, *The Complete Works of Brann, the Iconoclast* (1898)

"Vivandiere" is a French word for a woman assigned to a military regiment. I can't think of an occasion when I'd be inclined to use it, but if I did, I might be accused of being a **blatteroon**.

bloviate [BLOW-vee-ayt] (verb)

22

To write or speak windily and verbosely

"'I am reluctant to question Horace,' Natalia said, glancing nervously at the cuckoo clock. 'He has such a tendency to **bloviate**.'"

boanthropy [bo-AN-thruh-pee] (noun)

A mental disorder; the belief that one is a cow or an ox

"...Nebuchadnezzar may have been made to think himself a subject of **boanthropy** when 'he was driven from men and did eat grass as oxen,' continuing this occupation until his body was soaked with the dews of heaven, till his hair had grown like eagles' feathers and his nails like birds' claws."
—Frank Hamel, *Human Animals* (1915)

Moo! I'd rather be called a victim of **boanthropy** than a clumsy ox any day.

bombinate [BOM-bi-nate] (verb)

To hum or buzz

"The comedian, unless he wishes to **bombinate** in a vacuum—which is not the goal of the ordinary comedian's desire—can no more afford to be more immoral than he can afford to be more moral than his audience."
—Francis Henry Gribble, *Rousseau and the Women He Loved* (1908)

Some may find my attempts to **bombinate** a tune annoying—something I tend to do when nervous. Joseph Jordania, an evolutionary musicologist, has suggested that gentle humming and musical sounds relax humans. Yep.

bosk [bosk] (noun)

A small wooded area or thicket

"Laura felt mysteriously drawn to the dark **bosk** behind the house."

bricoleur [BREEK-o-lur] (noun)

One who engages in *bricolage* (construction by using whatever comes to hand or mind); a do-it-yourselfer

"A '**bricoleur**' engaged at the markets on any odd jobs that chanced to fall in his way, had noticed, during the long nights he passed waiting for a job, the negligence of these charbonniers, and made up his mind to supplant them."
—Charles Dickens, *All the Year Round* (1869)

My blogging is bricolage, a vertical patchwork of palaver and persiflage that leaks from my coconut almost every day. How's that for a mixed metaphor? As they say in the rulebooks, even if a mixed metaphor sings, it should be derailed.

My favorite science-fiction author, Philip K. Dick, favored bricolage. His print works, some of which are in the public domain and some are not, have been strip-mined by Hollywood's blockbuster machine, with mixed results, as any Dickhead will tell you. No doubt the man was a mad genius – and **bricoleur**. My favorite Dick book is the unfilmable (?) *VALIS*, a phantasmagorical mélange of sci-fi and gnostic speculation. What's not to like about an autobiographical novel that features a main character named Horselover Fat, a "plasmate," a child messiah, Valentinian Gnosticism, pre-Socratic philosophers, a rock musician named Eric Lampton, a "Black Iron Prison," and a pink laser beam from Sirius? In the fourth season of the TV series *L O S T,* a character can be seen reading a copy of *VALIS*. There. Bricolage.

bruxing [BRUKS-ing] (noun)

Nervous grinding and clenching of the teeth

"Desmond's incessant nocturnal **bruxing** drove his college roommate mad."

bumbershoot [BUM-ber-shoot] (noun)

An umbrella

"This umbrella has been in our family years, an' years, an' years. But it was

tucked away up in our attic an' no one ever used it 'cause it wasn't pretty."
"Don't blame 'em much," remarked Cap'n Bill, gazing at it curiously. "It's a
pretty old-lookin' **bumbershoot**."
—L. Frank Baum, *Sky Island* (1912)

This is a more common word than most of the ones included in this book;
I already knew what it meant before stumbling across it. I didn't know,
though, that there is a music and arts festival by that name that takes place
every year in Seattle. It rains a lot in Seattle, you see.

It rains in New Jersey, too, where I live, often with high winds, and my
own **bumbershoot** has blown inside out a few times, to the point that I
needed to buy yet another one. The umbrella is one of those inventions that
has never been quite perfected. Either that, or the manufacturers
deliberately make them too fragile to survive both wind and rain.
Sometimes I think I'd rather wear a rubbery yellow poncho or rain coat
with buckles, like I wore as a kid. I'd be uncool but dry.

buteonine [BYOO-tee-oh-nyne] (adjective)

Of, like or pertaining to buzzards

"Justina was offended by the **buteonine** swarming of so many distant
relatives after Uncle Cedric died."

C

caballine [KAB-uh-leen] (adjective)

Suitable for a horse

"'How do you expect me to swallow such a **caballine** tablet?' Mr. Hargreaves asked the bewildered pharmacist."

cachinnate [KAK-ih-nate] (verb)

To laugh loudly

"By no means is the wit of a kind to please the 'groundlings'; there is nothing of that 'capital fun' in it that so tickles the genuine John Bull, who, if he exerts his risible faculties at all, is satisfied with nothing less than a horse-laugh, which may be classical enough, because, we suppose, it was after that fashion that the centaurs of antiquity used to **cachinnate**."
—Antonius Anthus, in *The Foreign Monthly Review and Continental Literary Journal* (1839)

Things that make me **cachinnate**: bigfoot reports, possibly apocryphal George W. Bush quotations ("Too bad the French don't have a word for entrepreneur"), pro wrestling, *The Office* (meaning the TV show, especially the British version), and puns.

cacoethes [kahk-oh-EE-theez] (noun)

A mania, or an overwhelming desire; originally Latin

"We must talk, think, and live up to the spirit of the times, and write up to it too, if that **cacoethes** be upon us, or else we are nought."
—Anthony Trollope, *Barchester Towers* (1857)

"***Cacoethes** loquendi*" is a compulsion to talk or gossip. (That's NOT my problem. Ask anyone who knows me.) "***Cacoethes** scribendi*" is an irresistible itch to write. (That's me.) "***Cacoethes** weblogi*" is the obsessive urge to blog. (I made that one up.)

caitiff [KAY-tiff] (noun)

A despicable coward; a wretch

"When a bear cub wandered into the campsite, Professor Jones pulled the children in front of himself. 'Oh, you **caitiff**!' cried 10-year-old Penelope, the winner of the school spelling bee."

caliginous [kuh-LIJ-ih-nuss] (adjective)

Dark, misty, gloomy

"When by a just Nemesis the souls of men that are not heroically virtuous will find themselves restrained within the compass of this **caliginous** air, as both Reason itself suggests, and the Platonists have unanimously determined.
—Henry More, "The Immortality of the Soul" (1659)

In *The Wizard of Oz*, the Wizard, played by Frank Morgan, refers to the clinking, clanking Tin Man as a "collection of **caliginous** junk!" during a tour-de-force bout of C-word alliteration.

I'm not sure why the wizard would describe the shiny and chipper Tin Man as **caliginous**, but it's a great piece of alliteration. I used to think that "caliginous" meant something like "miscellaneous," which would make more sense in context. But it was Dorothy's dream, right? I guess she didn't know what it meant either.

callithumping [KAL-uh-thump-ing] (adjective)

Loud, noisy, boisterous

"It is conjectured that it is the intention of this structure to shelter the mob in rain and snow, so that the parson and the sick of the infirmary may have, despite of the weather, their daily **callithump**!"
—"Charlottesville Architecture," in *The Virginia Spectator* (1856)

I often think of "things" as stories. I sometimes feel like someone in a novel or film. I collect situations that I can write about. I get interested in certain people because they seem like characters to me—meaning they aren't *boring*. (Which doesn't mean they need to go around **callithumping**.) I guess I'm a writer.

candent [CAN-dent] (adjective)

Glowing because of, or as if from, intense heat

"A Single friend perhaps loiters behind the rest: you are alone in the house; you have just got upon a subject, delightful to you both; the fire is of a **candent** brightness; the wind howls out of doors; the rain beats; the cold is piercing! Sit down. This is a time when the most melancholy temperament may defy the clouds and storms, and even extract from them a pleasure that will take no substance by daylight."
—Leigh Hunt, "A Day by the Fire," in *The Reflector* (1811)

Obviously a fire can be described, poetically, as **candent**. But I've also seen heavenly bodies, like the Milky Way, so characterized. I've always wondered why our galaxy has to have a candy-bar name when most other heavenly bodies are named after mythological figures or eminent scientists. A **candent** candy bar would result in chocolate soup.

canorous [can-OR-uss] (adjective)

Melodious; musical

"The dull life at Oxford was varied by the occasional visit of a mesmeric lecturer; and one youth caused peals of **canorous** laughter by walking round in a pretended mesmeric sleep and kissing the pretty daughters of the dons."
—Thomas Wright, *The Life of Sir Richard Burton* (1906)

While I'm writing or editing, I like to listen to music. Not just any music. I listen to film scores, "ambient" music or jazz—music without lyrics, because it allows me to concentrate. I can choose to listen, or let the music function as white noise, depending on what I'm doing at the moment. I suppose that's the purpose behind Muzak, too, but elevator music annoys me. Its "calming influence" is just too damn manipulative. I think they play it in stores because it encourages people to buy more stuff—it tranquilizes any concern about spending too much. Or maybe I'm just paranoid.

Today, I've been listening to a beautiful, classic film score by the great Alex North: *The Long, Hot Summer.* It's from an old (1958) Paul Newman/Joanne Woodward movie based on some of William Faulkner's short stories. Very lyrical and literary and **canorous**—just the thing to listen to while editing a long treatise on financial conditions in Thailand. (No, I don't spend all my time writing about curious words.)

carriwitchet [KAR-ee-WIT-chet] (noun)

An absurd question, a pun, a quibble, a conundrum; a jocular or facetious comment

"I curse all squibs, crackers, rockets, air-balloons, mines, serpents, and Catherine-wheels, and can think of nothing and wish for nothing but laugh, gig, humour, fun conundrum, **carriwitchet**, and Catherine Clive!"
—David Garrick, correspondence to Mrs. Clive (1778)

So this hydrogen atom walks into a bar. He goes up to the bartender and orders a beer. He says to the bartender, "I think I've lost an electron." The bartender says, "Are you sure?" The electron says, "Yes, I'm positive."

So this carton of yogurt walks into a bar. He goes up to the bartender and orders a beer. The bartender says, "Hey, buddy, we don't serve yogurt in here." The yogurt says, "Why not? I'm a cultured individual."Etcetera, etcetera. That's **carriwitchet**.

catafalque [CAT-uh-fok] (noun)

A raised platform that a casket rests on during a funeral or memorial service

"I don't want a plain box," Renata said. "I want a sarcophagus on a marble **catafalque**."

catawampus [kat-uh-WOM-pus] (adjective or noun)

1. Askew, crooked, diagonal (adjective)
2. An imaginary wild animal (noun)

"[T]he circle is the most beautiful shape in nature. Young gentlemen seem to be aware of this, and by means of a material called hair they contrive to manufacture faces of all forms, from a perfect circle to a **catawampus** ellipse. If they want an elliptical face, they create a patch of hairs on the chin...."
—*North Carolina University Magazine* (1852)

Try to imagine what an animal called a **catawampus** might look like. I picture a swamp-dwelling creature that would be a cross between a lion and an octopus.

cavil [KAV-uhl] (verb)

To object in a trivial way or for trivial reasons

"Proved to me this day beyond **cavil** that it is not my material eyes which finally see, / Nor my material body which finally loves, walks, laughs, shouts, embraces, procreates."
—Walt Whitman, "A Song of Joys," in *Leaves of Grass* (1860)

Every weekend, I find a spider web in the same place in my backyard shed. I have to break it to get to anything in there, but it always comes back. I've started to feel sorry for the spider, but also impressed by its persistence. No, I do not **cavil**.

celeritous [sell-ER-it-uss] (adjective)

Quick, rapid

"There appeared in Forrest's right hand, which had seemed empty, which had seemed not to move or to perform in any **celeritous** and magic manner, a very small, stubby, nickel pistol, with a caliber much too great for it, and down whose rifled muzzle the earl found himself gazing."
—Gouverneur Morris, *The Spread Eagle and Other Stories* (1910)

I've never owned a gun myself, or felt any desire to. I did have a cap gun as a boy, but I don't think that counts. I liked it for the loud bangs and smell of gunpowder it made. So I would sometimes neglect the gun altogether and just explode the caps on the sidewalk by hitting them—**celeritously**—with rocks. Such fun! My late father did have a gun, a rifle, unloaded, in his bedroom closet. He used it to shoot woodchucks in our backyard. I never touched it, because it scared the bejesus out of me.

cete [seet] (noun)

A number of badgers together

"'Answer me now, lad, how would you say if you saw ten badgers together in the forest?'

'A **cete** of badgers, fair sir.'

'Good, Nigel—good, by my faith! And if you walk in Woolmer Forest and see a swarm of foxes, how would you call it?'"
—Arthur Conan Doyle, *Sir Nigel* (1906)

Of course, "badger" doesn't just refer to a burrowing mammal. It can also be a verb, meaning "to harass or annoy persistently"—as does my neighbor's fat mutt, which barks at me from behind a fence the whole time I'm out in the backyard. I think I'll get a squirt gun and shoot the cur in the face one of these days.

Of course, I'd rather deal with a noisy canine in my yard than a **cete**, any day.

chaogenous [kay-oh-JEE-nuss] (adjective)

Arising out of chaos

"The inferior gods, by whose agency the world was created, seem to be much the same as the **chaogenous** hero-deities of Hesiod and other ancient mythologists."
—George Stanley Faber, *The Origin of Pagan Idolatry* (1816)

I'm a believer in contained chaos. I stuff all my snail mail, junk and otherwise, into an antique roll-top desk in the living room, always with the intention of going through it and throwing all the flotsam away on the weekend. But I rarely get to it. Still, I know where to find it. When I open the desk, it all looks chaotic, but it's *contained*.

It's the same with my closet, which is too cramped to accommodate my entire wardrobe of dotcom-casual classics, not to mention some more formal attire. So I just throw the apparel that doesn't ever need to look as if it has met with a hanger or a drawer (like sweat pants) on the closet floor. It's a chaotic heap of garments, but it's out of site—contained. And, when the time comes, **chaogenous**. This is how I finesse my mess.

chaussure [sho-SUR] (noun)

Footgear; shoes

"'I delight in Hessian boots,' said Rebecca. Jos Sedley, who admired his own legs prodigiously, and always wore this ornamental **chaussure**, was extremely pleased at this remark...."
—William Makepeace Thackeray, *Vanity Fair* (1848)

I wear sneakers (athletic shoes, plimsolls) most days, as I work in a casual place. Sometimes I wear leather **chaussure**, though—no special reason—and feel a bit more grown up, if slightly less comfortable.

clinquant [KLING-kunt] (adjective)

Glittering, but in a false or cheap way, like tinsel

"No, there are too many of these fine sparks you talk of who perhaps may be very **clinquant**, slight, and bright and make a very pretty show at first, but the tinsel-gentlemen do so tarnish in the wearing, there's no enduring them."
—Thomas Shadwell, *The Virtuoso* (1676)

I once had a cat that liked to eat the tinsel (of the "icicle" type) off the Christmas tree. Maybe he had an iron deficiency. Anyway, he always threw it up later, in a **clinquant** hairball, which was both pretty from a distance and disgusting close up—like many things.

clishmaclaver [KLISH-muh-klay-ver] (noun)

Casual talk or gossip

"It was to this eminent minister that Daniel the Cricket would often betake himself, when he felt himself disposed for a little talk and **clishmaclaver**; and as at such times he had usually imbibed too freely of his favourite whisky, his conversation was not so edifying as was that of the Doctor."
—Cuthbert Bede, "Daniel the Cricket" in *Belgravia* (1879)

Let's see, do I know any good gossip? I know about a female friend (or ex-friend) of my wife's who was at one time in jail in Kentucky, of all places, on a drunk and disorderly charge. I know somebody who was recently on a "vision quest" in the Mojave Desert, according to a mutual friend (although I'm not sure the so-called quester would describe it that way). I know someone who's into S&M, but doesn't know that I know.... I often know a lot more **clishmaclaver** than people think I do. But I'll never tell.

conglobate [KONG-lo-bate] (verb)

To form into a globe or ball

"He decided to **conglobate** all of his string into a sort of weird planetesimal."

consanguinity [con-sang-WIN-ih-tee] (noun)

Relationship by blood or by a common ancestor

"**Consanguinity** forced Millicent to endure Martin's endless reminiscences of Christmases past."

consuetude [KON-swi-tood] (noun)

Custom; usage; habit

"Mr. Vanderhoople wanted to revive the old custom of tipping one's hat. Mrs. V then reminded him that he would first have to revive the ancient

consuetude of *wearing* a hat."

contortuplicate [con-tor-TUP-li-kayt] (adjective)

Braided or twisted

"....would you believe it? Wallich's and Griffith's plant driers were in the habit of pressing *once* in paper, and then spreading all out *in the sun:* no wonder their specimens are so **contortuplicate**."
—Joseph Dalton Hooker, in *Life and Letters of Sir Joseph Dalton Hooker* (1918)

One of the artist's studios I visited during a recent Jersey City Studio Arts Tour included some works that I found both fascinating and horrifying: constructions of found objects, cheap toys, plastic flowers, cast-off household objects, and all sorts of flotsam and jetsam, all **contortuplicated** together with wire into 3D assemblages. There were many, many of these compilations, some small and some large, all over the studio. They were accomplished works of art, but I couldn't help being reminded of a relative's house in California. She was a hoarder, and visiting her home was like walking around inside one of these agglomerations, which I at first assumed were the physical manifestation of a troubled mind. It was hard to see at first, but there was a kind of mad order to her placement of all the clutter. Madness or genius? It's often hard to decide.

coriaceous [kor-ee-AY-shuss] (adjective)

Having the appearance of leather

"After so many decades at sea, Captain Smyth's **coriaceous** face told a salty story, punctuated by two oceanic eyes."

corybantic [cor-uh-BAN-tik] (adjective)

Frantic, frenzied, ecstatic; the "corybants" were ancient worshipers of the goddess Cybele whose rites were celebrated with music and ecstatic dances. "It was as though the old Cornish giants had come back to life for a **corybantic** dance with the demirips of their race—dancing to the music of the sea sucking and gurgling into the caves at the base of the cliffs."

—Arthur J. Rees, *The Moon Rock* (1922)

"Demirips" is, I think, an alternate spelling of *demireps*. A demirep is "a person of doubtful reputation or respectability," according to TheFreeDictionary.com.

There were a lot of people dressed as demireps and acting like **corybants** on a Grammy Awards show I watched a few years ago. Music and singing seemed less important to the proceedings than flash and spectacle. There was even a circus act. I'd rather see and hear the stately Susan Boyle than some pop tart lip-syncing while dressed like a Vegas hooker and hanging upside down, at least on the Grammies.

coryza [kuh-RYE-zuh] (noun or adjective)

The common cold or its symptoms; sniffles

"'Visiting Pluto, are you?' Captain Spacewell asked. 'Prepare yourself for **coryza**-inducing temperatures.'"

Of course, Pluto isn't a planet anymore; it's been downgraded by astronomers to a dwarf planet, or minor planet. (I would prefer to call it a planetoid, because I like the sound of that.) It's a celestial snowball, probably with a rock in the center—the kind of thing the bully down the street threw at you when you were a kid, just because he hated your snowsuit. "**Coryza**" might be a good alternate name for Pluto.

cosmotellurian [cos-mo-tel-OO-ree-an] (adjective)

Pertaining to both heaven and earth

"'So, feet on the ground, head in the stars, eh?' said Mr. Dolty. The astronomer smiled patiently and said, 'I think of myself as a **cosmotellurian** investigator.'"

crepuscular [kri-PUSS-kyuh-ler] (adjective)

Of or like twilight

"After reading *Dracula*, the **crepuscular** sky filled George with dread."

cromulent [KROM-yoo-lent] (adjective)

Authentic, valid, fine or excellent

"The play, although not historically accurate, was **cromulent**, as was the story and acting."

I first encountered this word while reading, I know not why, a website called hotelchatter.com. It was describing a resort in Dalat, Vietnam, as "**cromulent**" and first-rate "whatever your French villa preference."

This word, which was coined by the writers (or a writer) of *The Simpsons*, seems to be seeping into the common language, and is already included in some online dictionaries. I'm not sure why we need it, but I like the sound of it. And one of the great things about the English language is that we have so many ways of saying the same thing.

By the way, what's *your* French villa preference?

cumberground [KUM-ber-grownd] (noun)

Something that is worthless—an object or a person

"'What a lot of **cumbergrounds**!' exclaimed Mrs. Woonsocket as she perused the antique shop's displays. But as her roving eye alighted on each gewgaw and gimcrack, it was obvious that this practiced derision was simply a prelude to another one of her expert haggling sessions."

Worthless people, taking up space? A number of reality-show "celebrities" come to mind. As for objects, they are almost too numerous to mention, right here in the room where I'm writing this. Almost but not quite. In one corner, we have an antique wheelchair containing a number of mismatched mannequin parts. On the mantelpiece, we have small replicas of the Eiffel Tower and the Space Needle, a Michael Jackson doll, and a fishbowl containing a single porcelain fish. The sideboard is covered with inherited bagatelles from my wife's deceased aunt's hoard, mostly odd costume jewelry. On the floor next to the fireplace, we have a teddy bear astride a miniature gargoyle. I could go on. But you get the point. I'm living in the

Museum of **Cumbergrounds**.

curwhibble [KUR-wib-ul] (noun)

A thingamajig or whatchmacallit

"Many thanks to your honor. What pretty **curwhibbles** and etceteras! I'll hang 'em to my watch to give it a travelled air."
—Anonymous, "A Captivity among the Rockites," in *The Metropolitan* (1831)

More junk. There are many objects around my home that one might call thingamajigs, whatchmacallits, or even **curwhibbles**. For example, something I found in a Chinese junk shop that hangs from a floor-lamp's switch. This whatsit has a little metal fan on top, from which is suspended an oddly shaped brass bell with some inscrutable writing engraved on it. And from that hangs a coin of some sort, with a square hole in the middle. There are bas-relief dragons curled around the hole, as if guarding it. And there are also red tassels hanging from various parts of this thing. I guess you could call it a bell, but it's much more than that. Altogether, when suspended, it's about 10 inches (25 cm) long. It is completely useless. And that's what I like about it.

cwm [koom] (noun)

A valley (originally Welsh; pronounced like "koom")

"Below a fertile **cwm** spread, with barns and the orchards of summer,
Behind, the terraced sides of a mountain, abrupt, in places rising high…."
—Walt Whitman, "Bivouac on a Mountain Side," *Leaves of Grass* (1865)

(Apologies to Whitman for the slightly altered quotation.)

Wow—a real word with no vowels. Welsh, with its minimal use of vowels, seems an odd language to me. My great-grandmother was from Wales, and we still have her leather-bound Welsh bible at my mother's house. The title is "Y Bibl." No letter E, which amused me as a kid. I thought it sounded like someone had translated the bible into alien baby talk.

cynosure [SIGH-nuh-sure] (noun)

A center of attention; an attraction magnet

"Ransom could see that, according to a phrase which came back to him just then, oddly, out of some novel or poem he had read of old, she was the **cynosure** of every eye."
—Henry James, *The Bostonians* (1886)

My favorite Henry James work is *The Turn of the Screw*, one of the few ghost stories that is truly scary and disturbing—because it's impossible to know exactly what is going on in the story. Is the **cynosure** in the story a ghost, or a figment of the imagination? Ambiguity can be more frightening than any monster.

D

dacoit [duh-KOIT] (noun)

A member of a gang of armed bandits

"The followings of the **dacoit** chiefs' gangs are made up partly of men who, like the leaders, are professional robbers. King Theebaw's method of dealing with such as came within his grasp was a simple one: if caught redhanded, they were usually crucified...."
—Parliamentary Papers, "The Conquest of Burma," in *The Edinburgh Review* (1887)

Watching a movie about Western **dacoit** leader Jesse James (*The Assassination of Jesse James by the Coward Robert Ford*) got me to thinking about guns. I've never owned a real one—just squirt guns, cap guns and an air rifle that shot ping pong balls. The only gun we have is my wife's glue gun, which she uses for her art projects. You can glue almost any two objects together with a glue gun. It's also quite easy to burn your fingers with one, so it might be of some use for self-defense at close range. It would be hard for a **dacoit** to hold up a train or rob a bank with a glue gun, however. You couldn't take it on an airplane. A gun is a gun.

deipnosophist [dipe-NAH-suh-fist] (noun)

Someone who is skilled in dinner-table talk

"Garvin's reputation as a **deipnosophist** almost made up for his notoriety as a cook."

deliquesce [del-ih-QWESS] (verb)

To melt, dissolve or become fluid

"They'll **deliquesce** like fungi, and keep a hundred eulogists mopping the spot where they left off."

—Henry David Thoreau, "A Plea for Captain John Brown," in *Anti-Slavery and Reform Papers* (1890)

There's a romantic scene in Salman Rushdie's novel *The Satanic Verses* in which a woman is said to "**deliquesce**" into a man's arms. I'm clearly not living in a Salman Rushdie novel. My life is more like this: My wife heaves an iceberg into the kitchen sink (she's defrosting the refrigerator), and I stand there making it **deliquesce** with hot water from the tap. Why? I don't know, but there is something meditative or even hypnotic about the process.

deliquium [del-IK-wee-um] (noun)

Melting or dissolution; liquefying; a maudlin mood

"When at length overtaken and reconveyed to the house, **deliquium** followed **deliquium**, and when they ceased, frenzy succeeded; the dark night of insanity had utterly quenched the light of reason."
—Reuben Percy, *The Mirror of Literature, Amusement, and Instruction* (1834)

"The worship of Odin astonishes us, — to fall prostrate before the Great Man, into **deliquium** of love and wonder over him, and feel in their hearts that he was a denizen of the skies, a god!"
—Thomas Carlyle, *On Heroes, Hero-Worship and the Heroic in History* (1840)

Things melt. The salad left too long in the refrigerator turns to green slime. A vinyl phonograph disc left in the sun warps disastrously. A plastic carafe left too close to the stove burner assumes a comical shape. All these things have happened to me, sad to say. But the worst was during my childhood, when my parents gave me a chocolate bunny one hot Easter morning. While we attended some religious rite, we left the confection in the car. When we returned, all that was left of my sacchariferous hare was a pool of chocolate milk. And yes, that put me in a **deliquium**.

deliriant [deh-LEER-ee-unt] (noun or adjective)

1. A poison which causes a persistent delirium, or mental aberration (noun)
2. Frenzied, delirious (adjective)

"The altered values of perceptive, elaborative, and active factors in these **deliriant** and intoxicant states thus run the gamut of excess and defect, combining in versatile permutations the several characteristics of the waking and the dreaming self."
—Joseph Jastrow, *The Subconscious* (1906)

Did you know that antihistamines are **deliriants**? My seasonal allergies were acting up one day, so I took some over-the-counter Loratadine (Rite Aid's antihistamine answer to Claritin). No hallucinations, no rabbits with pocket watches, but, thanks to cable news, I did see a square watermelon and a three-armed baby on TV.

desideratum [dih-sid-er-ATE-um] (noun)

Something considered necessary or highly desirable

"He was a man of simple tastes, and a cup of coffee—hot and black—was his only morning **desideratum**. Hers was a mocha coconut Frappuccino."

diegesis [die-uh-JEE-sis] (noun) **diegetic** [die-uh-JET-ik] (adjective)

A narrative; in film studies, the fictional world, milieu, or universe in which the story takes place

"'We're going to have to add some **diegetic** harpsichord to make that damn scene work,' the director mumbled."

That music you hear while watching TV or a film, which the characters in the story don't hear, serves a **diegetic** purpose: to tell you what you should be feeling or how you should interpret a scene on an emotional level. But you already knew that, right? Queue the wah-wah.

diluvial [dih-LOO-vee-ul] (adjective)

Pertaining to floods; brought about by a flood

"Moreover the Indian Ocean lies within the region of typhoons; and if, at the height of an inundation, a hurricane from the south-east swept up the

Persian Gulf, driving its shallow waters upon the delta and damming back the outflow, perhaps for hundreds of miles up-stream, a **diluvial** catastrophe, fairly up to the mark of Hasisadra's, might easily result."
—Thomas Henry Huxley, "Hasisadra's Adventure" (1903)

Thank heavens I've never had to deal with the consequences of an actual flood. The toilet backing up is enough of a **diluvial** disaster for me.

distichous [DIS-ti-kuss] (adjective)

Divided into two parts or two rows

"His eyes? Nor pen nor camera can present them. Imagine a black pearl imprisoning a diamond; imagine a dewdrop trembling on polished jet; add to these beauties *life*, and you will have the dormouse eye. His tail? **Distichous**, say the books. Feathers are mostly **distichous**, hair-partings are **distichous**, the moustache is **distichous**. So is the dormouse tail; but the hairs along it do more than merely part. They curl, upwards from the root, downwards to the point, and form a plume."
—Douglas English, *Wee Tim'rous Beasties* (1903)

Do you remember what the dormouse said? (It wasn't "feed your head.") In *Alice in Wonderland*, he said, among a few other things, "You might just as well say that 'I breathe when I sleep' is the same thing as 'I sleep when I breathe'!" He also told a story about three sisters who lived at the bottom of a treacle well and were learning to draw anything that began with the letter M. This confused Alice, who took everything literally, with comic effect. It's still one of my favorite books. Alice's story is **distichous**, of course, being divided into two parts: *Alice in Wonderland* and *Through the Looking-Glass*.

doolally [DOO-lol-lee] (adjective)

Insane, mad, or eccentric

"'I love talking to people who are a little bit **doolally**,' said Lisa. 'Not a lot crazy, just a little bit.'"

Much could be said about the **doolally** quality of the current machinations in Washington, D.C. An "absurd pantomime" was *The Economist*'s admirable phrase for it in a recent essay.

doxastic [doks-AS-tik] (adjective)

Of or relating to opinion

"'Please, no **doxastic** outbursts!' Professor Wisenhyme exclaimed as the chemistry students began to protest the experiment's sulfurous fumes. He took a deep breath. 'It smells like pure science to me.'"

E

ecdysiast [ek-DIH-zee-ast] (noun)

A stripper

"'You guys went to a strip club?' George's wife asked. 'No, no,' he said. 'We saw a performance by an **ecdysiast**.'"

I've never seen a live striptease act, but this word (coined by H. L. Mencken from the Greek word for molting) does bring to mind an odd experience I had several years ago, while walking down Eighth Avenue in Manhattan on a sunny afternoon. I saw a nude young woman walking on the opposite side of the avenue. She was not unattractive in shape, but her face wore a blank, zombie-like expression, as if she'd been hypnotized into naked perambulation. Astonished, I stopped to watch as this mesmerized **ecdysiast** sauntered down the block and then entered a brownstone. This event elicited some snickers from the other pedestrians, but not any commotion other than that. Only in New York.

edacious [ih-DAY-shuss] (adjective)

Voracious; devouring

"Abigail flailed in despair as the **edacious** aphids consumed her garden."

ejulation [ej-yoo-LAY-shun] (noun)

A wailing; lamentation

"'Eleven years of solitary confinement!' is the **ejulation** of Mr. Dickens, forgetting the crime for which the man was imprisoned!"
—Joseph Adshead, *Prisons and Prisoners* (1845)

I can't remember the last time I had an **ejulation**—probably when I stubbed my toe or bit my tongue. (I tend to cry on the inside.)

If you search for this word on Google Images, a lot of the resulting pix are pornographic (if "safe search" is off) for some reason. Perhaps some people think this word means something other than it does.

elanguescence [ee-lan-GWES-inse] (noun)

The soul's gradual loss of its powers

"Such a degree of reality might diminish by an infinite number of smaller degrees, and thus the supposed substance…might be changed into nothing, not indeed through decomposition, but through a gradual remission of its powers, or, if I may say so, through **elanguescence**."
—George Tapley Whitney and Philip Howard Fogel, *An Introduction to Kant's Critical Philosophy* (1914)

Having been around an alcoholic at one point in my life, I'm familiar with **elanguescence**. As James Brown said, "What we want—soul power! What we need—soul power!"

embrangle [em-BRANG-gull] (verb)

To involve in difficulty, conflict, disorder, or confusion

"Then there was poor Jacob Dodson, the half-witted boy, who ambled about cheerfully, undertaking messages and little helpful odds and ends, for everyone, which, however, poor Jacob managed always hopelessly to **embrangle**….They nicknamed him Jacob Doodle-calf."
—Thomas Hughes, *Tom Brown at Rugby* (1889)

A long time ago, my ambition was to be a magazine editor, and a certain non-profit organization offered me a job editing their quarterly magazine. I accepted, but it soon became clear that I had **embrangled** myself in a no-win situation. The organization turned out to be intensely bureaucratic, to the point that I couldn't make a single decision without the approval of several people, some of whom were not much interested in cooperating. It was a classic "responsibility without authority" situation, and eventually I was forcibly, uh, *disembrangled* from that gig. Just as well. Print periodicals are an endangered species, and cajoling pencil-pushers into making decisions they're afraid to be held accountable for is not my forte.

embuggerance [em-BUG-er-anse] (noun)

A small, annoying problem

"The ancient elevators in the Bon-Zai Building tended to stop on random floors, which Colin and Trevor found either an **embuggerance** or an amusement, depending on their mood and what they saw when the doors opened."

Some of my pet **embuggerances**:

~~~Going out for lunch with workmates and having to wait 30 minutes to be served.
~~~Opossums living in my backyard shed.
~~~My backyard apple tree shedding wormy, inedible apples that must be collected before I can mow the lawn.
~~~One of my zebras dying. (That's a type of tropical fish.)
~~~Our bathroom door sticking and having to be physically assaulted to close properly.
~~~Mice!

empery [EM-per-ee] (noun)

Absolute dominion, sovereignty, empire

"This may look like a crummy apartment to you, but it's my **empery**."

enantiodromia [en-AN-tee-oh-DROH-mia] (noun)

The tendency of things to change into their opposites

"The several parties project their unconscious upon each other, hence the mad confusion of ideas in every head. This is the **enantiodromia** that occurs in the individual life of man, as well as in that of peoples. The legend of the Tower of Babel turns out to be a terrible truth."
—Carl Gustav Jung, *Collected Papers on Analytical Psychology* (1917)

I have this ugly little plant, a type of orchid, that sits on the kitchen windowsill. It has dark, blade-like leaves and a lot of gnarled and twisted stems, but no flowers. I keep watering it, though, because I believe in **enantiodromia**. I'm hopeful that situations can change, if you can find the patience to wait long enough. Sure enough, it bloomed for a while last year. But after a week or so, it turned ugly again. I'm still watering it, though. I can wait.

ensorcell [en-SOR-sil] (verb)

To bewitch

"'You'll never **ensorcell** me,' said the skeptical Herbert. But the hypnotist soon had him dancing like a dervish."

entheomania [EN-thee-oh-MAY-nee-uh] (noun)

Abnormal belief that one is divinely inspired

"The king's **entheomania** was the root cause of his subjects' general woe."

enucleate [in-OO-klee-ayt] (verb)

To explain; elucidate

"'I will now **enucleate** the parameters of neuroimmunomodulation,' declared Professor Bourguignon to a sea of blank faces."

epizeuxis [ep-ih-ZOYK-suss] (noun)

Repeating words in succession; emphatic repetition

"**Epizeuxis** repeats immediately the same word; as, 'Ah Corydon, Corydon, what madness has seized thee?'"
—George Roberts, *A Catechism of Rhetoric* (1820)

Edgar Allan Poe was the master of this, as in "The Bells":

"....To the tintinnabulation that so musically wells
From the bells, bells, bells, bells,
Bells, bells, bells —
From the jingling and the tinkling of the bells."

Have you ever noticed that if you repeat a word enough, either aloud or just in your head, it ceases to have any meaning and just becomes a sound, or it starts to mean something other than you thought it did? This happens with names, too. As a child, when I was bored, I would sometimes engage in **epizeuxis**, repeating my name to myself until it became something else: my call, mic all, my kull, mycolgates, my call: eights.... I was a strange kid.

erinaceous [eh-rin-AY-shus] (adjective)

Like a hedgehog

"I felt no compunction about sticking a pig, if I could get near one, and all sympathy was for myself. To part company with your saddle, and to fall near these **erinaceous** brigands, is to be ripped from thigh to chin by their sharp tusks before there is time for rescue."
—Price Collier, *The West in the East From an American Point of View* (1911)

The one time I grew a little beard, I couldn't stop stroking my **erinaceous** chin like some evil mastermind plotting a global takeover.

escritoire [ess-krih-TWAR](noun)

A writing desk

"...this diverted suspicion into a new channel, and it was suggested that the robbery and the murder had really been committed by common housebreakers. It was then discovered that a large purse of gold, and a diamond cross, which the **escritoire** contained, were gone."
—Edward Bulwer Lytton, *Devereux* (1829)

Perhaps you are seated at an **escritoire** at this very moment. For myself, I prefer to curl up on the couch (also: sofa; grandma called it a "davenport") with my laptop as I tap my way along the information superhighway to my literary destiny.

Not that I don't have a desk. In fact, I have a few. My favorite is an antique roll-top desk with many shelves and cubby holes and secret compartments. If I had a traditional diary or a controversial will or some terrible secret committed to paper, I suppose that is where you would find it—if I happened to live in a Victorian novel. As it is, I use my **escritoire** as a repository for junk mail and miscellaneous missives from official sources: those scraps of paper everyone receives that are almost too dull to peruse but too important to recycle. The phrase "Save for tax purposes" has prevented many a tedious form from being reconstituted as bathroom tissue. Yes, if my roll-top **escritoire** could talk, it would have many a soporific story to tell.

esurient [ih-SOOR-ee-unt] (adjective)

Extremely hungry or greedy

"Whilst Yeats contemplates the lake and its water-fowl, **esurient** Edward devours huge loin chops, followed by stewed chicken and platesful of curried eggs, for he is suffering terrific qualms of conscience."
—George Moore, *Hail and Farewell* (1911)

This word doesn't just refer to an appetite for food; it can also refer to the libido. At the request of a (ahem) relative, we visited the Museum of Sex in New York, which is devoted to that sort of **esurience**. It's not a very big museum, and a lot of it is about animals. They have lots of chimp porn there, if that's your thing, and an interesting exhibition of Hollywood and indie film clips that deal with sex, either implicitly or explicitly. There was a whole genre of "nudie" films in the late 50s and early 60s that I never knew existed—all about nudist camps and lifestyle, featuring attractive people in the buff, but curiously unsexy. And you would have to be **esurient** to feel an attraction to the museum's creepy collection of life-size sex dolls, of both genders, that are more than correct, anatomically.

excerebro [ex-er-EE-bro] (verb)

To stupefy, make senseless, or bash someone's head in

"Professor Alamand proceeded to **excerebro** the class with his dull, repetitive lecture."

Watching the Academy Awards tends to have this effect on people. I was doing some challenging work on my computer while watching the Oscars one night, which may have prevented any loss of brain cells.

exergue [EK-surg] (noun)

A space on the backside of a coin that shows the date of engraving

"The rock on which Britannia is seated is cut off by a straight line, forming an **exergue**, in which is placed the date, 1860."
—*The Numismatic Circular*, Volume 15 (1907)

As a kid, I used to collect coins, and to this day I look at the **exergue** on almost every coin that's handed to me. I never find a very rare one, though. That's why I don't collect coins anymore.

exfluncticate / exflunctify [eks-FLUNK-ti-kayt] (verb)

To destroy completely

"Interrupted again! my blood boiled, and I resolved that I would do my best to '**exflunctify**' the animal at once."
—"Extract from the Journal of an Odd Fellow," in *The Parterre* (1834)

I used to watch a cable TV show called *Battlebots*, in which teams of engineers/nerds created actual robots that fought each other until one or the other machine was **exfluncticated**. There was something cathartic about it, and I didn't have to feel a bit sleazy, like I might if I were to flip the channel to, for example, professional wrestling. Whatever happened to the Battlebots of yesteryear?

eyot [ayt] (noun)

A small island

"Fog everywhere. Fog up the river, where it flows among green **aits** and meadows; fog down the river, where it rolls deified among the tiers of shipping and the waterside pollutions of a great (and dirty) city."
—Charles Dickens, *Bleak House* (1853)

No man is an island, but on a scale of one to ten, I've often felt like an **eyot**.

F

fanfaronade [FAN-fer-uh-NAID] (noun)

Empty boasting, arrogant bluster

"We laugh at the **fanfaronade** of the French, but never in my life did I see **fanfaronade** approaching in extravagance to the **fanfaronade** of this piece, and every burst of vapour was received by the audience with bouts of applause."
—"Diary of a Constant Reader," in *The London Magazine* (1826)

This word brings to mind the hilarious scene from *Monty Python and the Holy Grail* in which King Arthur battles the black knight, who continues his **fanfaronade** even after Arthur chops off his legs and arms. "It's just a flesh wound!"

fantods [FAN-tods] (noun)

A state of extreme nervous irritability

"He said we mightn't ever get another chance to see one, and he was going to look his fill at this one if he died for it. So I looked too, though it gave me the **fantods** to do it."
—Mark Twain, *Tom Sawyer, Detective* (1896)

Insects and other creepy-crawlies around the house give me the **fantods**. I don't even like to look at bugs. I take off my glasses before squishing them.

farraginous [fuh-RAHJ-uh-nuss] (adjective)

Composed of a variety of substances; a hodgepodge

"Thou art, I vow, the remarkablest progenitor barring none in this chaffering allincluding most **farraginous** chronicle."
—James Joyce, *Ulysses* (1922)

I once wrote a short story that was a **farraginous** amalgam of some paraphrased Charles Dickens, *Twilight Zone*ish dialog, and personal adventure. It was a success, I think; when I read it in public, I got some chortles and tittering from the audience in the right places, though it wasn't overall a comic piece, and some post facto compliments. Not bad for a hodgepodge.

farrago [fuh-RAH-go] (noun)

A medley or a conglomeration

"....every thing was collected that had been imported from the east relating to Osiris; and to that **farrago** was joined all that the Grecian rhapsodists had thought fit to invent, in order to amuse the credulous multitude."
—*Encyclopaedia Britannica* (1823)

My own personal **farrago** consists of the accumulated junk that covers the top of the chest of drawers in my closet. If I just swept it all into the trash I would never miss it, but I never get around to it. I'm sure it has something to do with the fact that each little treasure seemed worth saving at one time. And maybe they *are* worth saving. Maybe I'll put them into a coffee can and bury it in the backyard as a time capsule, so that future generations can study the sacred totems of our time: pennies, old keys, receipts, mints, Post-its with inscrutable messages, ties I never wear, and business cards for people I've forgotten.

festinate [FESS-tih-nate] (adjective, verb)

To move or act at high speed; hasty

"Advise the duke, where you are going, to a most **festinate** preparation; we are bound to the like. Our posts shall be swift and intelligent betwixt us."
—William Shakespeare, *King Lear*, Act III, scene vii (1623)

My mom has a dusty old upright player piano in her basement. I took a few piano lessons as a kid and used to practice on it. But I never liked playing the piano. I always preferred to insert a piano roll and let the thing play itself. It wasn't electric, though; I had to do some **festinate** pumping of the foot pedals to make it make it play "Melancholy Baby" or some other tin pan alley hit at the proper speed.

fissiparous [fih-SIP-er-us] (adjective)

Tending to break apart; divisive

"This endless multiplication of somatic cells has been going on under the eyes of numerous observers for forty years. What observer has watched for forty years to see whether the **fissiparous** multiplication of *Protozoa* does not cease? What observer has watched for one year, or one month or one week?"
—Herbert Spencer, "Professor Weismann's Theories," in *Popular Science* (1893)

The word "congress" means "coming together." Odd, isn't it, how **fissiparous** the U.S. Congress tends to be?

flâneur [fla-NER] (noun)

An idler, a dawdler or loafer; an idle man-about-town; a person who strolls about idly (originally French)

"For the perfect **flâneur**, for the passionate observer, it is an immense pleasure to choose his home in number, change, motion, in the fleeting and the infinite. To be away from one's home and yet to be always at home; to be in the midst of the world, to see it, and yet to be hidden from it; such are some of the least pleasures of these independent, passionate, impartial minds which language can but awkwardly define. The observer is a prince who everywhere enjoys his incognito."
—Charles Baudelaire, "The Painter of Modern Life," in *Le Figaro* (1863)

There are times when I'd like to think I could be the **flâneur** of the dictionary's definition: the idle, peripatetic stroller, appreciating everything around the city in a sort of moving meditation. But when I'm out walking around, I can't help speed-walking—even if I'm not in a hurry to get somewhere. People who walk slowly two or three abreast down the sidewalk ahead of me drive me crazy, until the concrete widens out enough for me to pass them. Then I feel a little silly, wondering if they think I'm trying to race them. I suppose some suburbanites have the same experiences in their cars—slow drivers ahead, so *honk, honk, honk.* Where's the fire?

flexuous [FLEX-shoo-us] (adjective)

Sinuous; winding or bending; serpentine

"Meanwhile Clare was meditating, verily. His thought had been unsuspended; he was becoming ill with thinking; eaten out with thinking, withered by thinking; scouraged out of all his former pulsating, **flexuous** domesticity. He walked about saying to himself, 'What's to be done - what's to be done?'...."
—Thomas Hardy, *Tess of the d'Urbervilles* (1891)

The most **flexuous** highway I've ever traveled was Route 1 in California. It's a twisty cliff-side thoroughfare with scary drop-offs—the ocean on one side and a sheer rock wall on the other, like something out of a *Road Runner* cartoon. The constant curves made me a bit carsick, but at least the drive up the coast was never boring: I feared we were about to plummet over the edge almost every minute, like that opening scene in *It's a Mad, Mad, Mad, Mad World.* The views of the Pacific were inspiring, though, so I recommend the route. Just don't eat first.

floccinaucinihilipilificate [FLOX-ih-NAW-sih-NIL-ih-PIL-if-ih-kayt] (verb—noun form below)

To judge something to be worthless

"....for whatever the world might esteem in poor Somervile, I really find, upon critical enquiry, that *I* loved him for nothing so much as his **flocci-nauci-nihili-pili-fication** of money."
—William Shenstone, letter, in *The Works, in Verse and Prose, of William Shenstone, Esq.* (1769)

Say it 10 times fast! Let me **floccinaucinihilipilificate**: Is there anything as worthless as a penny? I don't know why I keep jars full of them. I don't know why I pick them up off the sidewalk. They aren't even made of pure copper anymore, because that would make each one worth more than one cent, and people would melt them down, though the effort wouldn't be worth it, if you ask me.

flumadiddle [FLUM-uh-did-dul] (noun)

Utter nonsense or worthless frills

"More than that it is a confession of faith in the common sense of America, and a prediction that someday, somehow, we will turn from fol-de-rol and **flumadiddle** and once more conduct our affairs in a sane, common-sense manner."
—Arthur W. Park, *Public Service Management* (1922)

As I've written before, I approve of talking or writing nonsense, a most pleasurable activity—when done to entertain one's self or others, not to annoy. And of course, I also approve of slipping unusual lexemes into everyday conversations, as a social-science experiment, to see what kinds of reactions are received. For example, you might say "That was a very interesting **flumadiddle** you raised at the meeting today." Or: "I like that **flumadiddle** you're wearing! Where did you get it?" Please report back to me any blank look, inquiry as to your meaning, or sincere "thank you" you receive.

foofaraw [FOO-fuh-ra] (noun)

A great deal of attention paid to a trivial matter; much ado about nothing (various spellings)

"Beside, it goes against natur to leave bufler meat and feed on hog; and them white gals are too much like picturs, and a deal too '**foofaraw**'...."
—George Frederick Augustus Ruxton, *Life in the Far West* (1851)

Here's my **foofaraw**: The cord to my headphones is driving me mad. It kinks, it curls, it tangles, and twirls. I tried suspending the headphones upside down from a hook, thinking that gravity would straighten out my situation. But no, or at least not for long. I like to listen to... things... on the train while commuting, but I'm somewhat embarrassed to pull the headphones out of my man purse and start unknotting the cord while some slack-jawed passenger stares at me from across the aisle. The untangling doesn't go well. I fasten the headphones on, and instead of a nice, smooth, draping line I have an unholy snarl beneath my chin.

foudroyant [foo-DROY-unt] (adjective)

Dazzling, stunning

"The Amazing Zachary's **foudroyant** stunt drew gasps from the gawkers."

fraktur [frahk-TOOR] (noun)

A style of type: German black-letter text

"Okay, so you want the Halloween poster to have a scary, fascist vibe? Let's use **fraktur**."

Fraktur is that creepy Gothic/Germanic type often seen in the names of newspapers, such as *The New York Times*. Somehow, whenever I see it outside of the newspaper logo context, it always reminds me of Hitler. And I don't like being reminded of him. I used to wonder if there was anyone in the world today with the last name Hitler. Amazingly enough, if you search whitepages.com for that name, there are quite a few, both male and female, some of whom even sport the first name "Adolph." Life must be interesting for them.

frigorific [frig-uh-RIF-ik] (adjective)

Causing cold, chilling

"The reading public did not approve of it—the thermometer of popular opinion was down at 32, under its **frigorific** influence, so that we were abundantly justified in stuffing no more of Mr. Twitch's sonnets down the regurgitating throats of the literary multitude."
—Anonymous, "Treason," in *Blackwood's Magazine* (1821)

Hmm. Say "What a **frigorific** day," and people may think you're ecstatic about something.

frottage [fraw-TAHJ] (noun)

1. A visual-arts technique of obtaining an image by rubbing chalk, charcoal, graphite, etc., over a piece of paper covering a flat but 3D surface, such as a leaf
2. Sexual stimulation and satisfaction by rubbing against something, such as another human

"One day he was discovered, in a store, in the act of **frottage** on a lady. He was very repentant, and asked to be severely punished for his irresistible impulse.... he stated that at the sight of a noticeable posteriora of a lady, he was irresistibly impelled to practice **frottage**, and that he became confused and knew not what he did. Sent to an asylum."
—Richard Krafft-Ebing, Charles Gilbert Chaddock, *Psychopathia Sexualis* (1894)

"Posteriora"? Anyway, when I was a kid, I would sometimes create **frottage** by rubbing coins, leaves, etc., with paper and a pencil. It's hard to imagine, now, having the free, unstructured time to do something like that—just because I felt like it, not because I had to or someone told me to.

fulgent [FUL-jent] (adjective)

Shining brilliantly; radiant

"Unable to sleep, he wandered the hills that night, under the **fulgent** moon."

G

gaberlunzie [gab-er-LUN-zee] (noun)

A wandering beggar (originally Scottish)

"The **gaberlunzie** offered to sing for a copper, or to refrain from singing for two coppers."

galactophagist [ga-lact-o-FAY-jist] (noun)

A milk drinker

"Edwina was determined to raise a brilliant child. 'Here you are, my little **galactophagist**,' she said as she gave the baby his bottle."

gallimaufry [gal-uh-MAW-free] (noun)

A hodgepodge, a jumble, or a confusing medley

"Must your hot itch and plurisy of lust,
The heyday of your luxury, be fed
Up to a surfeit, and could none but I
Be picked out to be cloak to your close tricks,
Your belly-sports? Now I must be the dad
To all that **gallimaufry** that's stuffed
In thy corrupted bastard-bearing womb?
Why must I?"
—John Ford, *'Tis Pity She's a Whore* (1633)

That might be a good name for this book (**gallimaufry**, not "corrupted bastard-bearing womb").

gambrinous [GAM-brih-nus] (adjective)

Full of beer

"'Sorry, but I can't leave this party until I'm **gambrinous**,' Hector said. 'Even though I know I'll have to pay for it in the morning.'"

I sometimes have beer at lunch with co-workers. Me later that afternoon: **Gambrinous**? No. Slumberous? Yes.

Compare **potvaliant** in the P section. (No, it's not what you think— quite.)

gammerstang [GAH-mer-shtahng] (noun)

A tall, awkward woman

"'Every **gammerstang** needs her Pygmalion,' suggested Mr. Bosthoon, as Phoenicia glared down at him."

gasconade [gass-kuh-NAYD] (noun or verb)

Boastfulness, bravado, swagger; to boast

"Donald's incessant **gasconade** made Herbert feel two feet tall."

gelastic [jel-AS-tic] (adjective)

Provoking laughter

"Only Desmond's **gelastic** comments made the tedious seminar bearable."

ghoti [fish](noun)

Alternate spelling of "fish"

"'What's this on the menu?' Jordan asked. 'It says **Ghoti**.' 'I think they mean fish,' Sheila replied. 'The chef is a bit pretentious.'"

"Ghoti" can be pronounced like "fish":

gh, pronounced like "f" as in tough;
o, pronounced like "i" as in women; and

ti, pronounced like "sh" as in nation

glaikery [GLAY-kuh-ree] (noun)

Foolish behavior

"Oh! wad ye listen to a sound advice,
Ye'd quite yere **glaikery**, an' at last be wise...."
—James Duff, "Female Pride," in *A collection of poems, songs, etc., Chiefly Scottish* (1816)

"Only a fool writes for anything other than money," said Dr. Johnson. (That's Samuel Johnson [1709 - 1784], "arguably the most distinguished man of letters in English history," according to the *Oxford Dictionary of National Biography*, which I should keep by my bedside in case of insomnia.) The good doctor's quotation has been used over the years to discourage anyone from putting pen to paper without being paid, though of course it's absurd on the face of it. Samuel Johnson wrote plenty of letters for free, and he distributed a series of political pamphlets—more or less the blogs of the 18th century.

What is **glaikery** is to write without *compensation*, which doesn't have to be monetary.

gobemouche [GO-buh-moosh] (noun)

This word refers to someone who swallows flies. It can also refer to someone whose mouth is always open—a silly, gullible person or a boor. It's also the name for a type of bird.

"You dunno nuffin. You nuffin but one big fool ob a **Gobemouche**. I spec you nebber heerd dat we win de battle ob Bunker Hill—eh?"
—Albert Taylor Bledsoe, "The Gobemouchian Ideal of Government," in *The Southern Review* (1868)

A bug flew into my mouth once when I was a kid. I managed to spit it out, but the odd feeling stayed with me for a long time. "I know an old lady who swallowed a fly...."

godwottery [god-WOT-uhr-ee] (noun)

1. Elaborate gardening
2. The use of archaic language

"Verily, I say, 'tis most vexing to issue forth in antique jottings, as if from the honeyed pen of Shakespeare. One feels like an artless fly-bitten coxcomb! Or a lumpish doghearted wagtail! Or even an impertinent flap-mouthed dewberry! Fie on it! Methinks I must leave off with this gleeking, sheep-biting **godwottery**! Art thou in agreement?"

gongoozler [gon-GOO-zler] (noun)

An inquisitive bystander, often found by locks and other places where boats gather; a person who stares idly or curiously at something

"**Gongoozler**, an idle and inquisitive person who stands staring for prolonged periods at anything out of the common. This word is believed to have its origin in the Lake District of England."
—Henry Rodolph de Salis, *Bradshaw's Canals and Navigable Rivers of England and Wales* (1904)

Confession: Staring idly at something is one of my favorite hobbies. Now everyone can call me a **gongoozler**.

gormless [GORM-lis] (adjective)

Stupid, naïve, foolish, bone-headed

"Only she hadn't realized that for a girl of her sort, lovely and good-hearted and '**gormless**,' there's only one way of getting a fortune; namely, by marrying it."
—Berta Ruck, *His Official Fiancée* (1922)

I am very **gormless** sometimes, usually when I'm distracted. For example, I once drank some cleaning fluid that was kept in a water bottle that someone had put in the refrigerator; I don't remember why. I guess it had to be kept cool. Now, it might seem stupid in itself to put such stuff in a water bottle and keep it in the fridge. But the bottle was labeled "DON'T DRINK." As usual, though, I was thinking about work or some errand I needed to run, or a cult TV show or film, or some song was playing in my head. I just reached in, pulled out the bottle and took a swig—and spit it out, though I swallowed a little. Luckily it wasn't caustic, just terrible tasting. I didn't get sick, but I did make the further **gormless** mistake of telling someone what I had just done. I was called "absent-minded Michael" for about a week after that.

gossoon [go-SOON] (noun)

A boy; lad

"'I would never send a **gossoon** to do a man's work,' declared the erudite Mr. Webster. 'Or a baboon, either,' he whispered as Elmer stumbled into the room."

gowk [gouk] (noun)

A fool, simpleton or clumsy person

"Conceited **gowk**! Puff'd up wi' windy pride!"
—Robert Burns, "The Brigs of Ayr" (1786)

You might be a **gowk** and mistake this word for another: "gwok." According to the Urban Dictionary, gwok can mean "ugly"; it can also be a synonym for money. In Cantonese, it means "country." Hmm. An ugly money country. Suitable for **gowks**, no doubt.

gowpen [GOW-pen] (noun)

A double handful

"Lacking a cup, Gavin drank a **gowpen** of water from the stream."

gravid [GRAV-id] (adjective)

Pregnant, or full of eggs

"The gravest problems of obstetrics and forensic medicine were examined

with as much animation as the most popular beliefs on the state of pregnancy such as the forbidding to a **gravid** woman to step over a country stile lest, by her movement, the navel cord should strangle her creature."
—James Joyce, *Ulysses* (1922)

I don't have a beer belly, but if I did, I think I'd call it my grain-grown **gravidity** gut.

greige [graysz] (adjective or noun)

1. A color midway between gray and beige; taupe
2. A caucasian man who is attracted to Asian women
"'It's gray!' said Nadia, rubbing the fabric between her fingers. 'I can't wear a gray wedding dress!' 'No, it's certainly *beige*,' her mother replied. 'Call it **greige** and let me ring it up for you,' the saleswoman interrupted, with a note of desperation in her voice."

When you want something to fade into the background, you paint it **greige**, I suppose. I've always had a certain attraction to this color, which is no color. It "goes with anything," as my mom might say, though I admit it's a bit boring, like its components, gray and beige. (I had an old girlfriend who used to call the latter "blah beige.") It doesn't make a statement, so you don't have to worry about what anyone thinks of your khaki pants or oatmeal sweater. I don't quite understand the insulting (?) reference to white men preferring Asian women, though. (That definition comes from the Urban Dictionary.) Maybe it's because the women are neither white nor black. The guys can feel cool dating an Asian woman—not too conventional but not too radical. Chickens are often **greige**, aren't they?

H

habile [HAB-ihl] (adjective)

Generally able or adroit; handy

"Professor Allenby fixed the roof himself, and thought he'd proved '**habile**' with a hammer and nails. Then the first rains came."

haptic [HAP-tik](adjective)

1. Relating to or based on the sense of touch
2. Characterized by or favoring the sense of touch

"'You will please keep your hands to yourself,' Clara murmured to the **haptic** Mr. Weems."

hebetude [HEB-ih-tood] (noun)

Mental dullness or slowness

"The inept Mayor Smalltree's re-election would depend entirely on the **hebetude** of the townspeople, Malachi thought."

hesternal [hess-TER-nal] (adjective)

Of yesterday

"I passed up a side street, one of those deserted ways that abound just off the big streets, resorts, apparently, for such people and things as are not quite strident or not quite energetic enough for the ordinary glare of life; dim places, fusty with **hesternal** excitements and the thrills of yesteryear."
—Rupert Brooke, *Letters from America* (1916)

Compare **hodiernal**.

Speaking of the "thrills of yesteryear," I've taken to riding a bike in the local park in the evenings, something I haven't done—at least on a regular basis—since the **hesternal** days of my adolescence. It can be quite thrilling, what with all the other bikes, baby strollers, joggers, and urban hikers I have to share the byways with.

hircine [HER-sign] (adjective)

Of or characteristic of a goat, especially in strong odor

"He hesitated a moment: the landlady saw, calmly put down her work, and coming up pulled a **hircine** man or two hither, and pushed a **hircine** man or two thither, with the impressive countenance of a housewife moving her furniture."
—Charles Reade, *The Cloister and the Hearth: A Tale of the Middle Ages* (1922)

My **hircine** astrological sign is Capricorn—the goat. I have felt like "the goat" at times, although I don't eat tin cans.

hobbledehoy [HOB-uhl-dee-hoy] (noun)

A gawky, awkward youth

"Young Alec hated being called a teen-ager (too 'corny,' he said) or an adolescent (too 'clinical'). '**Hobbledehoy**!' he said one day while perusing the dictionary. "That's what I am!" He promptly scribbled the word down the length of his leg cast."

hodiernal [HO-dee-UR-nul] (adjective)

Of the present day

"Credit me, fairest lady," said the knight, "that such is the cunning of our English courtiers of the **hodiernal** strain, that, as they have infinitely refined upon the plain and rustical discourse of our fathers, which, as I may say, more beseemed the mouths of country roisterers in a May-game than that of courtly gallants in a galliad, so I hold it ineffably and unutterably improbable, that those who may succeed us in that garden of wit and courtesy shall alter or amend it."

—Sir Walter Scott, *The Monastery: a Romance* (1820)

The **hodiernal** era—what shall we call it? The latter half of the 20th century was called the "post-war era," referring to World War II. We're a bit beyond that now, aren't we? Same for "cold war era." I've heard it said that we are in a "post 9/11 era," but as earthshaking as that event was, I don't think it can define us for decade after decade. I suppose you could say we're in a second Elizabethan era, but that may be too specifically British a reference. Whatever we call the current times we're living through, they're obviously profoundly transitional. Call it the Age of Confusion. Strange days indeed.

hoghenhine [HA-gehn-hyne] (noun)

A member of one's family; a guest who stays more than three nights

"As to guests, we will that every one uncouth, answer for his guest that he shall have harboured for more... than two nights together, so that the first night he shall be deemed a stranger and uncouth, the second night a guest, and the third night a **hoghenhine**."
—Francis Morgan Nichols, *Britton* (1865)

I suggest that you NOT refer to your family members or long-term guests as **hoghinhines**, at least not in their presence, unless you are angry with them. They might take it the wrong way.

honeyfuggle [HUN-ee-FUG-uhl] (verb)

To deceive with flattery or sweet-talk

"'Look here, Malone,' said the sheriff, as he drew a pistol, 'you know damned well what's over thar, an' thar ain't no use in tryin' ter **honeyfuggle** me. The sooner you own up the better it'll be fur you.'"
—Opie Percival Read, *Len Gansett* (1888)

I'm trying to imagine what would happen if I used **honeyfuggle** in conversation with mixed company. I think I might be misunderstood. Or even slapped.

honorificabilitudinitatibus
[ON-or-IF-ick-a-bill-ih-TOO-din-ih-tat-EE-bis] (adjective)

With honor

"O, they have lived long on the alms-basket of words.
I marvel thy master hath not eaten thee for a word;
for thou art not so long by the head as
honorificabilitudinitatibus: thou art easier
swallowed than a flap-dragon."
—William Shakespeare, *Love's Labor's Lost,* Act 5, Scene 1 (1598)

In the context of the play, this odd passage from Shakespeare seems to be a bit of sarcasm aimed at a pedant—someone who might use a word like **honorificabilitudinitatibus**. A flap-dragon was (is?) a flaming raisin, used in a game in which people grabbed raisins out of a dish of burning brandy and extinguished them in their mouths before eating them. What fun!

hooroosh [who-ROOSH] (noun)

An uproar, a great fuss

"What a **hooroosh** aloft there! I would e'en take it for sublime, did I not know that the colic is a noisy malady."
—Herman Melville, *Moby-Dick* (1851)

Near where I work in Newark, New Jersey, there's quite a **hooroosh** on Wednesday afternoons: a huge outdoor karaoke party, complete with a stage and concert amplification. The Otis Redding manqué (look that up!) I recently saw hit most of the notes.

humdudgeon [hum-DUD-jun] (noun)

An imaginary illness

"Whenever there was work to be done, Zachary took to his bed with a **humdudgeon**."

hypnoetic [hip-noh-ET-ik] (adjective)
Pertaining to logical but unconscious mental processes

"When Horace said he would 'sleep on it,' we knew the problem was about to be solved, thanks to his **hypnoetic** talents."

hypnopompic [hip-noh-POMP-ik] (adjective)

Associated with the period between sleep and wakefulness

"....knowledge of Mrs. Finch's balloon ascent had been acquired supernormally by Mrs. Thompson… and had lain dormant in her subconsciousness until awakened by a natural association of ideas set in motion on her reading about the accident to the airship, and not even then emerging into her full consciousness, but emerging only in a **hypnopompic** dream."
—J. G. Piddington, "Phenomena in Mrs. Thompson's Trance," in *Proceedings of the Society of Psychical Research* (1904)

This word brings to mind the **hypnopompic** period I experience most mornings between tumbling out of bed and gulping down my first cup of coffee. While I'm staggering around like Boris Karloff in *Frankenstein*, I'm often brooding over some bizarre or disturbing event—until I realize that "oh...that was just a dream."

hypocorism [hi-POK-er-ih-sim] (noun)

A pet name, or baby talk by an adult

"A classic **hypocorism** originated from the French endearment *mon petit chou:* 'My little cabbage,' returned Madame, 'we are so near to ruin as we are, that a step or two nearer is of no importance.'"
—Leonard Merrick, "Little Flower of the Wood," in *Metropolitan Magazine* (1907)

These days, even if you're French, I do not recommend that you refer to your loved one as "my little cabbage." Not unless you want to do a lot of explaining.

My mother had a **hypocorism** for me when I was a tot: "Pumpkin." Why she called me that I do not know. I could ask her, but it would be awkward—I don't think she knows either. I certainly didn't resemble a pumpkin or gourd of any sort. At least she didn't call me a little cabbage.

I

illapse [ill-LAPS] (noun or verb)

To fall or glide into, the act of falling or gliding into something

"What moves thee, if the senses stir not? Light/Moves thee from Heaven, spontaneous, self-inform'd;/Or, likelier, gliding down with swift **illapse**/By will divine."
—Dante Alighieri, *The Divine Comedy*(1555)

Hmm, gliding into something.... I recall driving a Volkswagen on a gusty winter night in upstate New York and gliding off the road into a snow bank. Car, passenger, and driver were unharmed in this **illapse**.

imbroglio [im-BRO-lee-o] (noun)

A confusing, complex, or embarrassing situation, a painful misunderstanding, or a scandal

"Mr. Ervin Wardman, in the *Broadway Magazine* for April, exhaustively reviews the McClellan-Hearst-Murphy **imbroglio**, and concludes that Mr. Hearst's real ambition, the goal of his desire, is the White House."
—Albert Shaw, *The American Monthly Review of Reviews* (January–June 1907)

This is a pretty easy word, compared to most of the ones I'm foisting upon you. I more or less knew what it meant without looking it up—no **imbroglio** when I encountered it in the quote above.

impecunious [im-pih-KYOO-ni-us] (adjective)

Poor; penniless

"It began with a contribution from the first **impecunious** painter in payment of an overdue board-bill, his painting being hung on a nail beside the clock. Now, all over the walls...are pinned, tacked, pasted and

hung...sketches in oil, pastel, water color, pencil and charcoal...bearing the signature of some poor, stranded painter, preceded by the suggestive line, 'To my dear friend, the landlord.'"
—Francis Hopkinson Smith, *The Veiled Lady* (1907)

I always seem to be **impecunious**—that is, penniless—when I'm in the check-out line and the cashier rings up a sale price with a "1" or "2" on the end. It's only as I'm stuffing a handful of the resulting change in my pocket that I remember that big jar of pennies at home on my dresser.

incalescence [in-kuh-LESS-inse] (noun)

The action or process of heating or becoming hot

"Though we could hear the teapot's **incalescence**, there was no one in the kitchen."

incunabulum [in-kyoo-NAB-yoo-lum] (noun)

A book printed before the 16th century; artwork from an early period

"Ethan described his first book as an '**incunabulum**,' though it had been out of print for only two years."

"Finally, an **incunabulum** may have an aesthetic value. The early printers were craftsmen in every sense of the word."
—Pierce Butler, "A Typographical Library," in *The Papers of the Bibliographical Society of America* (1922)

I attend an antiques fair every summer in upstate New York near my mother's house. There are many old books on sale there—though not as old as **incunabula**. The aroma of musty, falling-apart books invokes the past like nothing else, I think. Nostalgia reeks.

infrangible [in-FRAN-jih-bul] (adjective)

Unbreakable; not violated

"Hearts will never be practical until they can be made **infrangible**," said the

Wizard. The Tin Man was riveted, but could only say, "Huh?"

ingurgitate [in-GUR-ji-tayt] (verb)

To gulp or swallow greedily

"But what purpose does this wealth serve? Do they use it as a means for benefiting society? Is it employed as a sword with which to defend the weak? Is it an architect that builds? Is it a seed-sower that distributes? Or, is this quality merely the capacity to take in—to **ingurgitate**, ingurgitate, ingurgitate?"
—Henry Ward Beecher, "Remnants," in *The Original Plymouth Pulpit* (1871)

We have a bird feeder hanging from the apple tree in our back yard. The free food has attracted flocks of small, ravenous birds (chickadees and sparrows, I think), as well as the occasional red cardinal and blue jay. They fight over the seeds, and **ingurgitate** so fast that they end up dropping a lot of them onto the ground, where fat squirrels scarf them up. It's quite a pig-out session, until the neighbor's cat strolls through the yard; then they all scatter until she leaves. I wish I had a video camera and could capture these wildlife vignettes. To me, it's far more entertaining and edifying than anything on Animal Planet.

invidious [in-VID-ee-us] (adjective)

Offensive, causing ill will or resentment

"….the leisure of the leisure class is still in great measure a predatory activity, an active assertion of mastery in which there is enough of tangible purpose of an **invidious** kind to admit of its being taken seriously as an employment to which one may without shame put one's hand."
—Thorstein Veblen, *The Theory of the Leisure Class* (1912)

Whenever I find myself making an **invidious** comparison between myself and someone else, I think of this quotation:"The fundamental delusion of humanity is to suppose that I am here and you are out there."
—Yasutani Roshi

iqueme [IH-qway-may?] (adjective)

Pleasing or agreeable

"The **iqueme** distinction about living in a metropolis, as opposed to the country, is that one can walk to find just about any necessity. And I do."

According to the website wordnik.com, **iqueme** is not a valid Scrabble word, which isn't very **iqueme**, is it?

I can't find a reference for how to pronounce it. Is it "eye-cue-me"? "ick-ew-may"? "I-cweem"? If I was an audiobook narrator, I'd be in trouble. It's hard to imagine what sort of book such a word would appear in, though. Apparently, it's Middle English. But that's all the more reason to resurrect it in your daily conversation, gentle readers. Pronounce it however you like, though if you say "I-cweem" someone might think your saying "ice cream":

"That perfume you're wearing is so **iqueme**."
"Ice cream?"
"Yeah, you know, delicious."

ishkabibble [ISH-ka-bib-ul] (noun? adjective?)

It has various meanings: "don't worry," "a silly person," "nonsense," or as an expression of surprise. It was also the stage name (as Ish Kabibble) of the late comedian Merwyn Bogue. The word was originally spelled "ishgebible."

"The customary '**Ishgebibble**' attitude will mark both occasional intermittent worshippers and them who get religious inspiration by absent treatment."
—Emil G. Hirsch, *The Reform Advocate* (1920)

Search for **ishkabibble** online and you'll find odd references, including a racehorse with that name, a restaurant called Ishkabibble's Eatery in Philadelphia, and a "Turtleneck blouse with ruffles recolored by ishkabibble"—a clothing designer, I'm guessing, not the late comedian.

As a kid, I went through a period of wearing turtlenecks. I think I wanted to be futuristic, like a *Star Trek* crewman. I don't know why it's so often assumed that people in the future will wear turtlenecks (or mock turtlenecks) all the time. It's **ishkabibble**! That type of shirt has been around at least since the 1800s.

J

jacal [huh-KAHL] (noun)

A thatched-roof hut

"Crawling on hands and knees where the brush was low, they at last came within range of the crazy-looking **jacal**, that, in the whiteness of the moonlight, made a black spot on the side of the hill. A dark figure crouched within the hut…."
—Louise Wasson, "On the Divide" (1899)

I have a little thatched roof partial **jacal** at home, over our internal kitchen window. My wife made it from thatch and bamboo sticks for a party with a beach theme we had one winter. We liked it so much that we kept it. No, we don't drink mai tais under it.

jackanapes [JAK-uh-nayps] (noun)

An impudent or impertinent person, especially a young man

"John stuck his tongue out at Mr. Wagstaff. 'Quite the little **jackanapes**, aren't you?' Wagstaff asked. 'I don't go by *Jack* and I ain't no ape!' John hissed."

jaculate [JAK-yoo-lait] (verb)

To throw or hurl

"'I found the ball,' Kevin said. 'Hey, let's go out back and **jaculate**!' 'Uh, no…. I, uh, have a girlfriend, dude,' said Jerry."

janizary [JAN-uh-sair-ee] (noun)

A follower or supporter

"'Will you be my **janizary**?' Mayor Sprague asked Millicent at the rally. 'Sir, I'm a married woman!' she replied, turning several shades of red."

jargogle [JAR-gog-uhl] (verb)

To confuse or mix up

"Whether all you say have any thing more in it than this, I appeal to my readers: and should willingly do it to you, did not I fear, that the jumbling of those good and plausible words in your head 'of sufficient evidence, consider as one ought,' &c. might a little **jargogle** your thoughts...."
—John Locke, *Letters Concerning Toleration* (1689)

Things that **jargogle** me:

~~~I'm looking for something, and my wife tells me it's "in the closet." We have eight closets in our house. "Which closet?" I ask. "The Closet!" she yells.
~~~Kids playing in the street when there are two huge parks a couple of blocks away in either direction
~~~A relative who has changed her first name to something different— but not legally; trying to remember and use it
~~~High fructose corn syrup
~~~Weekend train schedules
~~~midlife
~~~vesting (financial, not sartorial)
~~~PPOs vs. HMOs
~~~Variations on your basic zebra: zebroids (something that resembles a zebra), zorses (zebras crossed with horses), zebrules (zebras crossed with mules), zonies (zebra ponies), zonkies (zebra plus donkey), donkras (donkey plus zebra) and zebra hinnies (same as a donkra)

jeremiad [jer-uh-MY-ud] (noun)

A long lament or complaint, or an angry harangue, derived from the name of the Hebrew prophet Jeremiah

"Yes, a **Jeremiad** is needed. But not Mr. Noyes's kind of Jeremiad. For the whole effect of his Jeremiad is that we are going to the dogs, and that there is absolutely nothing good in free verse."
—Edmund Kemper Broadus, "The Lunatic, the Lover, and the Poet" in

The Canadian Forum (1922)

Who's Afraid of Virginia Woolf is one of my favorite plays. I even wrote a paper about it in college—or a few papers, if I recall. It can be analyzed from several angles: political, Freudian, rhetorical, dramatic, etc. But what makes it an exciting verbal tour de force is that the main characters, George and Martha, engage in a knock-down, drag-out **jeremiad**.

jobbernowl [JAH-bur-nowl] (noun)

A blockhead, a stupid person

"Mr. Dour yelled '**jobbernowl**!' and slammed down the phone. It was yet another wrong number."

K

kakistocracy [kak-ih-STOK-ris-see] (noun)

Government by the worst, least qualified or most unprincipled

"Is ours a government of the people, by the people, for the people, or a **kakistocracy** rather, for the benefit of knaves at the cost of fools?"
—James Russell Lowell, "Letter to Joel Benton" (1876)

I e-mailed this word and definition to actor/activist Janeane Garofalo during the George W. Bush presidency, and she read it on her radio show. Somehow, this word didn't catch on with any other pundits, though.

kelemenopy [kell-uh-MEN-oh-pee] (noun)

A straight-line sequence through the middle of everything, leading nowhere

"In ancient sailors' fearful imaginations, ships that sailed in a straight line toward the watery horizon would fall off the edge of the world, in a voyage of **kelemenopy**."

A straight line to nowhere. Things seem to be sailing along smoothly, and then they get interrupted. Derailed. Cut off. Somebody dies, a job ends unexpectedly, people vanish, your favorite TV show gets cancelled before all the plot threads unspool. The ship hits an iceberg. Like the time my old Mustang broke down in the middle of the Brooklyn Bridge. Like the time I got "laid off" from my magazine editing job. Like the novel I abandoned because I couldn't figure out how to end it: **kelemenopy**. But sometimes you have to reach nowhere ("now here") in order to figure out how to start over again.

kerfuffle [ker-FUFF-uhl] (noun)

A fuss, commotion or disturbance

"'What a **kerfuffle**!' Mrs. Talbot exclaimed as the gentlemen's disagreement devolved into a brawl."

killcow [KIL-kow](noun)

An arrogant or bullying person

"'Don't be such a **killcow**,' Helen said when Karl kept interrupting her. 'What do you mean?' he replied. 'I'm a vegetarian!'"

kipple [KIP-uhl] (noun)

Useless trash, junk, or rubbish; coined by the science-fiction writer Philip K. Dick in his book *Do Androids Dream of Electric Sheep*

"'I have to clean up this room,' said Hiram. 'Irrelevant **kipple** seems to multiply around me like rabbits in heat.'"

A friend writes: "Someone I live with is, alas, a **kipple** collector. We have a very full basement full of so-called art materials, plus broken lawnmowers, lamps that don't light, unpacked boxes from our move several years ago, etc.—none of which I'm allowed to dispose of without bringing down the wrath of God on my person. And now the **kipple** is metastasizing from the basement into other areas of the house."

All I can suggest is this: Andy Warhol famously said that junk should be packed in a box with a date on it, and if you haven't opened the box within a year, you should just throw the box away—without looking inside. More and more, I think he was right.

klangfarbe [KLANG-far-buh] (noun)

Instrumental timbre or tone

"Chloe lived to play the flugelhorn. 'Nice **klangfarbe** you have there,' Charles said after she played a trill. 'No!' Chloe exclaimed. "I keep telling everyone—it's a flugelhorn!'"

kohl [kohl] (noun)

A cosmetic used to darken the eyelids; think Cleopatra or Johnny Depp as Jack Sparrow, not the former German chancellor

"423. A small wooden Toilet Box with five compartments to contain the black powder called **Kohl,** used to blacken the eye-lids as in the days of Jezebel."
—Henry Abbott, *Catalogue of a Collection of Egyptian Antiquities* (1853)

I suppose in a pinch, a modern Jezebel could use coal (fossilized carbon) as **kohl.**

kthxbye [kay-thangks-BY] (adjective, adverb, interjection, noun, verb)

Okay + thanks + good-bye

"After a while, Herbert began to feel more tolerated than welcomed at the party, and he said **kthxbye.**"

"**Kthxbye**" is a sort of mash-up of those auto-phrases we all tend to use so cavalierly. It's used a lot when leaving a voicemail, I've noticed. Why do people think they need to cut off the message abruptly at the end with "**kthxbye,**" enunciated at hyper speed before (metaphorically at least) slamming down the phone? It's not like the tape is going to run out on the answering machine anymore. Let's all say good-bye to this word. Okay? Thanks.

Seriously, you never know when it's going to be the last time. All correct. Thank you. God be with you.

L

labeorphily [lay-bee-OR-fil-ee] (noun)

Collection and study of beer-bottle labels

"Confronted with the huge number of empties by the back door, Wilbert blamed his obsessive **labeorphily**."

lachrymose [LAK-rih-mohs] (adjective)

Mournful or tearful

"Her tears seemed to grieve the kind-hearted Munchkins, who became **lachrymose** and began pulling out handkerchiefs."
—L. Frank Baum, *The Wonderful Wizard of Oz* (1900)

A variation on this word is:

lacrimation [LAK-rih-may-shun] (noun)

Secretion of tears, especially in excess

"Once again, Billy's team lost, and the whole city was filled with **lacrimation**."

lagniappe [LAN-yap] (noun)

A small gift presented to a customer with a purchase

"'Welcome to Burger Land. May I take your order?' Sid said, mechanically. 'Yes, my child,' said Nigel. 'I would like one of those children's meals that includes a **lagniappe**, please.'

"Sid sighed and rolled his eyes. 'I'm sorry,' he said. 'We don't serve Chinese food here.'"

It's funny about gifts. I don't care much about receiving them anymore. If I want something in the nature of a physical object (within reason), I can often get it for myself—exactly the way I want it. It's much better than relying on someone else's taste. I get more pleasure out of giving... not necessarily material things, but things like music files or information or recommendations. It may not be reciprocated, but what the hell. I don't let it make me lachrymose. Nobody gives Santa Claus anything, not even a **lagniappe**, and he's a "right jolly old elf."

lamprophony [lam-PROF-uh-nee] (noun)

Vocal loudness and clarity

"Robert decided to order a fruit crepe for dessert. 'A creep? A crap?' his five-year-old son demanded to know, with embarrassing **lamprophony**. Robert imagined all the Euro-yuppies in the restaurant staring and snickering. 'It's sort of like a big Pop Tart,' he hissed. 'Now keep your voice down.'"

Some people are in love with the sound of their own voice. Some deserve to be, being mellifluous enough to go pro with their utterance; others are just loud. When I can hear every word you say, even if there is a thick wall between us, you need to turn down your **lamprophony**. This means you, semi-detached neighbors who apparently conduct demented exorcisms next door.

legatee [leg-uh-TEE] (noun)

A person who receives a legacy (a bequest, an inheritance) in a will

"'You don't,' said Mr. Pecksniff, with a melancholy pressure of his hand, 'quite understand my nature yet, I find. No, Sir, I am not a **legatee**. I am proud to say I am not a legatee…. And yet, Sir, I was with him at his own request. *He* understood me somewhat better, Sir. He wrote and said, 'I am sick. I am sinking. Come to me!' I went to him. I sat beside his bed, Sir, and I stood beside his grave. Yes, at the risk of offending even *you*, I did it, Sir.'"
—Charles Dickens, *Martin Chuzzlewit* (1844)

Dickens was a genius at making up odd, rather comical Anglo-Saxon names: Martin Chuzzlewit, Mr. Pecksniff, Mr. Pickwick, Alfred Jingle, Augustus Snodgrass, Mr. Bumble, Vincent Crummles, Wackford Squeers, Dick Swiveller, Mr. Toots, Betsey Trotwood, Uriah Heep, Honoria Dedlock, William Guppy, Joshua Smallweed, Mrs. Jellyby, Herbert Pocket, Nicodemus Boffin, and of course, Ebenezer Scrooge.

How would you like to go through life with a name like Wackford Squeers or, heavens, Dick Swiveller? I suppose if you were a wealthy **legatee** named William Guppy, Jr., for example, you could shrug it off. But imagine the playground teasing. I wouldn't mind having a distinctive name like Nicodemus Boffin, though, instead of the common one I share with thousands across the nation, some unsavory.

lexiphanic [lex-ih-FAN-ik] (adjective)

Pretentiously verbose

"For an elucidation of this cloudy system, and as a model of agricultural fine writing, see the **lexiphanic** report of three eminent wise-acres, employed by the Duke to survey this gentleman's farm, carried on by scuffling."
—Woburn Beds Abbey, *Woburn-Abbey Georgics; or, The Last-Gathering* (1813)

When you're an editor (of text), you're always aiming for precision and felicity while avoiding both oversimplification and verbosity. At the same time, you have to preserve the author's "voice" (assuming there is one). In a way, it's like topiary or, better, hairstyling, when the owner of the bush asks for "just a trim." It has to be the same, but shorter and better. On my blog, I sometimes wax **lexiphanic**, when it amuses me. Wax? I don't mean beeswax.

lickspittle [LIK-spit-ul] (noun)

A fawning underling, a toady

"Mr. Maus was thrilled by his appointment as the department's manager, until he discovered that 'the Big Cheese' wanted nothing more than a **lickspittle** in the position."

loganamnosis [LAHG-an-um-NOH-sis] (noun)

A mania for trying to recall forgotten words

"The password continued to escape him. 'I just can't shake my **loganamnosis**,' Bill said with a sigh. 'Have you seen a doctor?' Sam asked worriedly."

luciferous [loo-SIF-er-us] (adjective)

1. Bringing or providing light
2. Providing insight or enlightenment

"I therefore take the liberty to say, that I do not regard meteoric light as due to the presence of a **luciferous** atmosphere belonging to the meteorite itself; for I cannot believe that any appreciable quantity of ether or of inflammable gas could be confined around such small bodies, or retained by their feeble attractive power after they come in conflict with the air."
—Daniel Vaughan, "A Catalogue of Observations of Luminous Meteors" (1858)

One of the most essential things I brought with me on a recent vacation was a flashlight—a rechargeable flashlight with a bulb **luciferous** enough to illuminate an entire room. It proved handy on the night we blew a fuse at the hotel in London (which was more like a B&B) by trying to plug in a power strip with our U.S. outlet adapter. (The electrical system is different in England.) The hotel was flummoxed by this turn of events; the doltish French desk clerk said they had to call in an electrician. (Just to replace a fuse or flip a circuit-breaker switch?) So we spent a night without power, except that my **luciferous** "torch" enabled us to find our pajamas, brush our teeth, and get into bed without bumping into the furniture.

M

macroverbumsciolist [mac-ro-verb-um-skee-OH-list] (noun)

A person who is ignorant of large words, or a person who pretends to know a word, then secretly refers to a dictionary

"'I'm feeling cantankerous,' Austin said. Garrick smiled and said nothing. It occurred to Austin that Garrick had no idea what he meant. 'Cranky, I mean,' he said. 'You know—testy, ornery, grouchy....'

'I am not a **macroverbumsciolist**,' Garrick said, dourly. 'Triple word score!'"

I only use online lexicons these days, but I still have a superannuated, ponderous, chunky, crimson, hardcover copy of the *American Heritage Dictionary*, for whenever I'm feeling like a **macroverbumsciolist**. It resides under the mouse pad adjacent to our decrepit desktop computer. I'm thinking of hollowing it out (the dictionary) and using it to store oddments, jetsam, and old View-Master reels.

makebate [MAYK-bayt] (noun)

A person who creates discord or conflict

"'I am no **makebate**, no inciter of quarrels,' said Nelson. 'I simply think that a discussion of one's religion shouldn't be taboo in polite company.'"

marplot [MAR-plot] (noun)

A stupid and officious meddler whose interference compromises the success of any undertaking

"As each project dissolved into chaos, Ethan's predicament became agonizingly clear: he was working for a **marplot**."

mattoid [MA-toyd] (noun)

A semi-insane person

"'That man,' said the Doctor in a low, earnest voice, 'is a **mattoid**.'
'A what?' said the Vicar.
'A **mattoid**. An abnormal man. Did you notice the effeminate delicacy of his face? His tendency to quite unmeaning laughter? His neglected hair? Then consider his singular dress...'
The Vicar's hand went up to his chin.
'Marks of mental weakness,' said the Doctor."
—H.G. Wells, *The Wonderful Visit* (1895)

I loved reading Wells' science-fiction novels as a kid, especially *The Time Machine,* the full text of which can be found online. It still seems like the most perfect science-fiction novel ever, to me. I'm a **mattoid** for it.

meaching [MEE-ching] (verb or adjective)

Hiding, skulking; cowardly

"Lord, Bill! what a trembly, knock-kneed, **meaching** sort of a husband she's a-going to fashion to her hand, one of these days! But pretty? None more so. And a-going all to waste out here in the desert!"
—John Breckenridge Ellis, *Lahoma* (1913)

We've all done it. You see someone you don't want to see approaching, and you duck behind someone else or pretend to be preoccupied and oblivious. You're **meaching**!

mendacious [men-DAY-shuss] (adjective)

False, dishonest, lying, or untruthful

"And then she would say quite simply, without taking (as she would once have taken) the precaution of covering herself, just in case, with a little fragment borrowed from the truth, that she had at that very moment arrived by the morning train. These words were **mendacious**; at least for

87

Odette they were mendacious, insubstantial, lacking (what they would have if true) a basis of support in her memory of her actual arrival at the station; she was even prevented from forming a mental picture of whatever quite different thing she had been doing at the moment she pretended to have been alighting from the train."
—Marcel Proust, *Swann's Way, Remembrance of Things Past* (1913)

I ride the PATH commuter train back and forth every day at rush hour, but I never think of myself as "alighting" from it—more like charging out of it with the rest of the herd. My life is not very Proustian, though I have a pretty good memory of "things past," including the time I tried to read Marcel's book. I thought his long and winding sentences were elegant, but I found the endless accumulation of thousands of them to be soporific. (Note to self: use "soporific" in conversation. *Resist* temptation to be **mendacious** and say "grinchy" if someone asks what you mean.)

mesonoxian [mez-oh-NOX-ee-an] (adjective)

Pertaining to midnight

"His **mesonoxian** thoughts kept Sam wide awake in bed, his head feeling like a hall of mirrors, reflecting an unceasing cavalcade of the previous day's predicaments."

As a confirmed night owl, my bedtime is often **mesonoxian**, if not post-**mesonoxian**. Morning coffee is my salvation.

metagrobolize [met-uh-GROB-oh-lyze] (verb)

To confuse, perplex

"We simply hung about deck, moping, oppressed, bored and **metagrobolized**, none breathing a word to the other. Pantagruel lay slumbering on a stool, close to the upper cabin, a copy of Heliodorus in his hand."
—François Rabelais, *Gargantua and Pantagruel* (1567)

I'm confused. Is "Heliodorus" a book or an author, François? Probably a human. According to Wikipedia (source of all wisdom), there were umpteen ancient Greeks and Romans with this name. Only one of them, I have discovered, has a fan page on Facebook, however: Heliodorus of Emesa, whom ten people in the Book of Faces "like." (Not me; I don't warm up to people quickly, especially if they've been dead for two millennia.)

Heliodorus wrote a novel called *Aethiopica*. Now, as an auspicious English major, I was taught that "the novel," as we know it anyway, was invented in the 18th century, not in ancient Greece, so this so-called novel was probably more like an epic poem, à la the *Iliad* or the *Odyssey*, except it's described as a "romance," the story of "Theagenes and Chariclea." I'm guessing they were like Romeo and Juliet in togas. The only reason I know about *Aethiopica* at all is that it also has a fan page on Facebook, well-liked (more than four times more liked than the author himself) by a throng of 44 Facebookies. I'm tempted to "like" it even though I've never heard of it before, let alone read it. "Michael likes *Aethiopica*" would indubitably get my 215 Facebook friends **metagrobolized**.

minatory [MIN-uh-tor-ee] (adjective)

Menacing or threatening

"He was often observed peeping through the bars of a gate and making **minatory** gestures with his small forefinger while he scolded the sheep with an inarticulate burr, intended to strike terror into their astonished minds."
—George Eliot, *The Mill on the Floss* (1860)

I observed a sheep being sheered once, at a state fair. The animal was scared and made a weird, keening sound—the sheep equivalent of a scream. Those huge, noisy electric clippers were **minatory**, to the sheep, which is something I occasionally think about when I wear wool.

misodoctakleidist [miss-uh-DOC-tah-KLAI-dist] (noun)

Someone who hates practicing the piano

"Unable to progress past 'Chop Sticks,' Tatiana had to admit to being a **misodoctakleidist**. 'That's it,' she thought, 'I'm selling this baby grand and buying a player piano.'"

I took piano lessons from a neighbor for a short time as a kid, but I was a **misodoctakleidist** and gave it up, which I sometimes regret. I was too immature at the time to commit to it, but part of it was also that my family's piano was in the gloomy, dusty basement of our house, which wasn't conducive to long sessions of tickling the ivories. Another problem was that it was an upright, non-electrified player piano, and I was always tempted to stop practicing scales, insert a piano roll, and start pedaling. It played a jaunty version of "Melancholy Baby," I remember.

misoneist [miss-uh-NEE-ist] (noun)

Someone who hates change or innovation

"We suspected that poor Great Grandpa had been reading the dictionary again. 'Call me a **misoneist**,' he said, 'but let me keep my Victrola!'"

mondegreen [MON-duh-green] (noun or adjective)

A mishearing of a phrase, so that it acquires a new meaning

"'I realize now you said to *ping the tall man*,' Norton explained. 'And that does make sense, if you mean I should contact our boss. But I heard it as *pay the toll man*. I like that **mondegreen** better. It sounds a bit Dylanesque, don't you think? Pay the toll, man, to cross the River Styx.'"

I mishear song lyrics all the time. For years, I thought it was "sweet Loretta Modern" in the Beatles song "Get Back," and I was disappointed to find out later that this was a **mondegreen**. It's actually "sweet Loretta Martin." I still like my version better, and I think it makes more sense in the context of the song.

mooncalf [MOON-kaf] (noun)

A freak or monster; a fool, a daydreamer

"Instead of a purse or a bubble, which incloses the foetus, there was a globulous body like a **moon-calf**, or false-conception, which contained nothing organized, and which being opened presented nothing different

from a **moon-calf**, nothing that was any way formed or regularly disposed...."
—Anonymous, "Of the Formation of a Chicken in the Egg" in *London Magazine* (1752)

I live pretty close to the ocean, though not close enough to always be aware of it. I like the sound of waves crashing, and I even used to listen to a CD of that to get to sleep at night when things were noisier around my house. Call me a **mooncalf**, but I still listen to it occasionally, with headphones, even when not trying to sleep. It's hard to feel anxious or depressed, or concerned about the past or the future, when you can hear ocean waves in your head, heaving.

mooreeffoc [MOOR-ee-fok] (noun or adjective)

Something that appears strange when seen from an unusual angle

"That wild word, '**Moor Eeffoc**,' is the motto of all effective realism; it is the masterpiece of the good realistic principle—the principle that the most fantastic thing of all is often the precise fact."
—G.K. Chesterton, *Charles Dickens: A Critical Study* (1906)

This word comes from Charles Dickens, who used it in his abandoned autobiography. He was sitting in a London cafe one day and noticed that "moor-eeffoc" is "coffee room" spelled backwards; Dickens was looking at the establishment's name from the "wrong" side of the window. G.K. Chesterton and J.R.R. Tolkien later used "**mooreeffoc**" in print to mean something suddenly seen in a strangely new way. (You might say that David Lynch films are full of **mooreeffoc** places, objects, and people.)

It's one of those words that is more commented on than used, but I feel up to the challenge: "Her face transformed into a frightening **mooreeffoc** as he looked up from the floor, with her spiked heel pressed firmly against his chest." Sadly, I'm no Dickens.

morigerous [mor-IHJ-er-us] (adjective)

Obedient, compliant, submissive
"A robot should be **morigerous**," grumbled Captain Spacewell when he

learned of the android mutiny.

mulct [muhlkt] (noun or verb)

1. A penalty or fine
2. To defraud

"We, nevertheless, for your unhallowed intrusion upon our councils, believe it our duty to **mulct** you and your companion...."
—Edgar Allan Poe, "King Pest" (1835)

When you're a freelancer, no employer is deducting taxes from your paycheck, so you're supposed to pay income taxes to the federal government quarterly, or face a bit of a **mulct** in April, when everybody pays their taxes, for being late. As a full-timer who does a little freelancing on the side, I don't bother to pay quarterly, though. The **mulct** isn't big enough. Maybe if the Feds threatened me with a few hours of jail time instead, I'd be more motivated to do their bidding.

mumpsimus [MUMP-suh-muss] (noun)

Someone who adheres to old ways that are obviously wrong

"The best of the joke is, that Johnston, who seems here to have deserted for a moment the old **mumpsimus**, contradicts himself in the very next page, and having laughed at 'broken' metaphors in one breath, attempts, in the next, to 'reduce' one, after a manner of surgery almost as awful as that of Warburton himself."
—T. D., "On the use of Metaphors" in *Blackwood's Edinburgh Magazine,* (1825)

Hmm. Who might we apply this word to? I'm thinking of a certain **mumpsimus** from a certain political party. Maybe you are, too, even if it isn't the same party. That's politics.

munted [MUHNT-ed] (adjective)

Broken, peculiar, abnormal, or drunk
"That night, he dreamed about opening the box again. There was a **munted**

cup inside, a broken ceramic mug with something written on the side in a jagged font: 'I have too much blood in my caffeine system.' He picked it up and took a long, delightful sip. It was the most delicious cup of coffee he had ever tasted."

Munted... blood... As a kid, I used to get spontaneous nosebleeds. I would wake up in the middle of the night sometimes, wondering why my pillow was wet. I would turn on the light and discover that I had been lying in a puddle of my own blood. Icky—and **munted** in a way, in the sense of peculiar. I would sometimes get them during the day, at school, too, and would have to go to the nurse's office and lie down for a while, squeezing my nose with a tissue. It was very inconvenient and embarrassing.

To this day, I don't know what caused them, but they were more frequent in the winter, so it may have had something to do with my nasal passages drying out too much in the cold, desiccated air. I haven't had a nosebleed in years, but every time I experience some post nasal drip I still half expect to look down and see a **munted**, red blotch. (I know, I know: "Thank you for sharing, Michael.")

myrmidon [MUR-mih-don] (noun)

Someone who carries out, without question or ethical qualms, a master's orders

"'Abduction!' gasps the Doctor. 'Heu! Heu!'
'Yes! In my agitation I forgot to mention it—but do you know the address of the house in which that roué Kelsey's **myrmidon** said your child would spend the night?'"
—Archibald Clavering Gunter, *The Man Behind the Door* (1904)

Abduction.
One of my wife's friends, who we haven't seen in a while, told us that she was abducted by...them. The aliens. Only she didn't like the words "abducted" or "abduction" or "abductee." She preferred to call herself an "experiencer." She didn't think of her experience (whatever it was) as negative, or not entirely. She also refused to give us any of the details, having apparently been instructed not to by "them," becoming a **myrmidon** in that respect. She was a painter, and she gave us a small

painting with little images of flying saucers subtly mixed into the color fields. She also included a phrase in tiny letters in one corner of it: "They are us."Whatever that means.

N

nephelococcygia [NEF-el-o-kok-SIJ-ee-uh] (noun)

Cloud gazing; the act of looking for and finding shapes in clouds; also, when capitalized, the name of "Cloud-Cuckoo-Land" in Aristophanes' *The Birds*

"Terrence spent Saturday prostrate in the yard and in **nephelococcygia**, finding inspiration in the thunderheads."

I remember seeing a lot of things in clouds as a kid: faces, cities, fabulous beasts. I can't do that anymore, which is sad. Now I just see water vapor, though I still can't quite believe, sometimes, that I couldn't sit on one of those diaphanous thrones if I could just get up there.

neroli [NER-uh-lee] (noun)

An essential oil distilled from the flowers of the orange

"The origin of the term '**neroli**' applied to the otto of orange-blossom is not very definite. It may have been named after the celebrated Roman Emperor Nero, who was so fond of scents that he caused the roof of his dining halls to represent the firmament, and to shower down, night and day, all sorts of perfumes and sweet waters."
—George William Septimus Piesse, *The Art of Perfumery* (1867)

I'm not sure I'd want to dine while perfume, however sweet smelling, fell from the ceiling. Night and day?

I read an article about the late author David Foster Wallace, one of my favorites, which listed the words he circled in his dictionary, including **neroli**. He may have just liked the sound of it—and maybe he also knew that **neroli** oil is used in aromatherapy as an antidepressant, which is something he definitely needed. It's also said to be a hypnotic, aphrodisiac and a euphoric—sort of a citrus equivalent to Ecstasy.

nescience [NESH-unss] (noun)

Ignorance; agnosticism

"'Your **nescience** never fails to impress me,' Abigail cooed whenever Mr. Dumas offered yet another of his outrageously ill-informed opinions. He would then grin at what he assumed was her admiration."

I refuse to be an agnostic. I'm more of a heretic. I believe God is something like the "force" in *Star Wars*, not like Zeus or the sky deity with the cranky personality described in the Bible. I also believe the historical Jesus had no intention of founding a new religion, and that most of the stories about him are metaphors. Tell me I'm wrong, sailor. Tell me this is **nescience**.

nihilarian [NYE-hih-lar-ee-an] (noun)

One who deals with useless or unimportant things, or is engaged in trivial activities

"At loose ends after his assignment ended, Caleb became a **nihilarian**, spending each day starting and then abandoning crossword puzzles, walking aimlessly around the neighborhood, and polishing the silverware."

"**Nihilarian**" would be a splendid name for a blog like mine, or maybe "**nihilarity**." Blogging may seem useless, but I used to scribble *ad nauseum* in an actual diary, which nobody read except me. Truly **nihilarious**, because I couldn't stand to read it—and still can't. I tend to be an extreme solipsist when writing only for myself. Or talking to myself—a transcript of that would be a word salad with pine-nut dressing.

ninnyhammer [NIN-ee-ham-er] (noun)

A fool, simpleton or silly person

"You silly, awkward, illbred, country sow...have you no more manners than to rail at Hocus, that has saved that clodpated numskull'd **ninnyhammer** of yours from ruin, and all his family?"
—John Arbuthnot, "The History of John Bull" (1712)

Sometimes I think I'd have to be a **ninnyhammer** to collect all of these obscure words. I've been doing it for years, without a clear idea of what I would do with them. Then one day I realized I could collect them in a book, achieving fame and fortune. The rest is history.

nisus [NYE-suss] (noun)

Effort; endeavor; exertion; impulse

"Surprising everyone, Alphonse, with great **nisus**, did a headstand. 'Clears my sinuses,' he explained."

nosism [NO-siz-um] (noun)

The practice of referring to oneself in the plural, as "we"

"We so rarely fall into the mistake of puffing the *Literary Gazette*, that we ought to be excused now and then in the indulgence of that agreeable **nosism**."
—*The London Literary Gazette* (1831)

Mark Twain once said, "Only kings, presidents, editors, and people with tapeworms have the right to use the editorial 'we.'" I inhabit one of those categories (no, I don't have a tapeworm, although I am mysteriously hungry at present); I don't use the editorial "we" much, however. **Nosism** has its charms, though, and it expresses a certain verity. As Walt Whitman said, "I am large, I contain multitudes." Don't we all?

nudiustertian [noo-dee-uss-TUR-shin] (adjective)

Of or relating to the day before yesterday

"When I hear a nugiperous Gentledame inquire what dress the Queen is in this week; what [is] the **nudiustertian** fashion of the Court; with egg to be in it in all haste, whatever it be; I look at her as the very gizzard of a trifle, the product of a quarter of a cipher, the epitome of Nothing, fitter to be kicked if she were a kickable substance than either honored or humored."
—Nathaniel Ward, *The Simple Cobbler of Aggawam* (1647)

As I write this, the day before yesterday was Sunday. I used to go to church on Sunday, but I'm too much of a heretic now. Sunday feels like the last day of the week, even though it is the first. Sunday, traditionally, was a "day of rest," but that's Saturday for me—the day I sort of collapse and do things that amuse me. On Sunday, I do my errands, my shopping, my scheming for the week ahead. I abhor Sunday, if only because of that horrible feeling that the weekend is rapidly draining away. Oddly, I don't mind Mondays as much, despite my **nudiustertian** longing.

Oh, "nugiperous"? Ward liked to coin words. It means "ridiculous," I think.

nullibicity [nuhl-ih-BISS-it-ee] (noun)

The state of being nowhere (the opposite of ubiquity); nonexistence

"I had a desk, a chair, some bookshelves, a computer and a printer, a plug-in coffee pot, and clients who insisted on **nullibicity**."

The Holy Grail, the Fountain of Youth, a perpetual-motion machine, cold fusion—many "things" are **nullibicities**, but people keep searching for them. Could it be that the search or the *wanting* is the point, that the seekers wouldn't know what to do with themselves if they actually reached the goal one day?

nutation [noo-TAY-shun] (noun)

A nodding of the head

"The audience's collective **nutation** convinced the dramatist to cut the fifteenth act."

O

obambulation [oh-bam-byoo-LAY-shun] (noun)

To wander aimlessly or walk about

"At last I made a halt in my **obambulations**, and, addressing a merry-faced maiden who stood at the kitchen-window, inquired when the 'old fellow' would be at home."
—"Pictures of My Barrack Life" in *New Monthly Magazine* (1851)

If I had the prerogative to do as I pleased each weekday, I would engage in a good deal of gallivanting around the city I live in, camera in hand. Indeed, many of the photographs I take result from just such perambulatory traipsing on Saturday or the Sabbath. Urban hiking is agreeable; wandering in the woods is even more so. What appeals to me about **obambulation** isn't so much the specific scenery but the feeling of autonomy—and the serendipity.

obdormition [ob-dor-MISH-un] (noun)

Numbness, or the tingling felt when a limb is "asleep"

"Then my leg fell asleep, so I made ambitious circles with my feet, like a nervous orangutan, to cure my **obdormition**."

Yeah, I hate limping around when my foot falls asleep; don't we all? Sometimes, late at night, I just wish my head would fall asleep.

oblomovism [uh-BLAW- mahv-is-em] (noun)

Indolence, apathy, indifference or laziness

"'No,' the lady quickly replied, 'it is not indolence that I mean. It is not **Oblomovism**. The defect is more positive than that.'"
—Lydia Lvovna Pimenoff and Edmund Noble, *Before the Dawn* (1901)

I'm sitting on the couch as I type this, after a long day of chopping trees and sawing lumber (metaphorically speaking), and the pull of **oblomovism** is almost irresistible. In fact, I think I will—

obnubilate [ob-NOO-buh-late] (verb)

To becloud or obscure

"The witness's long, discursive answers served to **obnubilate** the issues."

obtenebrate [ob-TEN-eh-brayt] (verb)

To darken or place in shadow

"...thus do I return to you, dearest Ingeborg, to lay my head upon thy bosom, that thou mayst fan away the vapours which **obtenebrate** my soul, whilst placing thy warm hand upon my heart."
—Fredrika Bremer, *The Rectory of Mora* (1845)

Just before a thunderstorm on a hot August day, the wind rises and the whole world **obtenebrates**. I love that moment.

octothorpe [OCK-toe-thorp] (noun)

The name for a telephone keypad symbol, also called the pound symbol: #

"It was a slow day at the pet store, and as the birds screamed and the puppies squealed, Sebastian stared at the telephone keypad, hoping that Fatima would call. Pound symbol or **octothorpe**? Which was correct? In the end, did it matter?"

oggannition [og-GA-ni-shun] (noun)

Snarling or growling (also spelled ogganition)

"She snored so loudly that her roommates mistook the cacophony for **oggannition**."

Almost every time I walk past a neighbor's house, a tiny, ugly dog—some kind of pug—on the sill behind the front window goes into a paroxysm of **ogganition**, snarling and yapping at me while running back and forth and jumping up against the glass. I believe this little monster would tear me apart if it could only get at me. The poor creature is bored, I suspect, and wishes I would try to break in, so it could chomp on my leg. I just smile at Pugsley (my imagined name for him/her), which accelerates the frenzy. Long after I've passed on by, I can still hear the **ogganition**, with what I detect is an edge of disappointment in each yip and yap.

oikofugic [oy-ko-FU-jik](adjective)

Marked by the urge to wander or travel away from home

"Genevieve's employment as an air hostess for Oceanic Airlines enabled her to indulge her most **oikofugic** fantasies, but an emergency landing in Uzbekistan was not one of them."

I'm a fan of wandering—but whatever its pleasures, after a while it makes you appreciate your little hovel on Familiarity Street again. Ultimately, I need a routine, which you can't establish while traveling, to feel grounded. Although... too much routine leads to complacency and **oikofugic** boredom. That's when it's time to pack up and perambulate again. Breathe in, breathe out.

omphalos [OM-fuh-luss] (noun)

1. The navel
2. A center

"'You have the cutest **omphalos**, surfer dude,' she said coquettishly. He cocked his blond head, grinned and said, 'How do you know?'"

omphaloskepsis [om-fuh-lo-SKEP-sis] (noun)

Navel-gazing, or preoccupation with oneself

"As the grass grew waist high and the weeds bloomed, Victor seemed a victim of procrastination. But it was more that he preferred

omphaloskepsis to yard work."

My little brother had an "outie" bellybutton as a kid, the subject of much **omphaloskepsis**, and I used to press it while saying "ding dong!" as if it was a doorbell. He would laugh.

oneiric [oh-NYE-rik] (adjective)

Related to or suggestive of dreams

"A fairly common type observed was a state of mental confusion associated with what has been termed **oneiric** delirium, symptoms of which were associated with a history of concussion and exhaustive experiences."
—John H. W. Rhein, M.D., "Psychopathic Reactions to Combat Experiences in the American Army," *The American Journal of Insanity* (1920)

The **oneiric** John Lennon song "#9 Dream" is often rattling around inside my head.

onolatry [oh-NOL-uh-tree] (noun)

Worship of asses (donkeys!)

"Nietzsche has depicted the leaders of the nineteenth century as engaged in a veritable **onolatry**."
—Irving Babbitt, *Rousseau and Romanticism* (1919)

My mother lives in the country, in upstate New York, and from her backyard, you can see two donkeys behind a fence in a neighbor's yard, the beneficiaries of **onolatry**, I assume. ("Nice ass!" we've been known to say.) Sometimes we feed them cookies when we visit. They seem to prefer ginger snaps.

oojah [OO-zsah] (noun)

A whatchamacallit, a thingumabob

"Portia had been ruminating for weeks over what to name her 'junk shop,' as she referred to her second-hand gift store. Then it came to her. '**Oojah**,' she whispered, as she fondled a lamp made from a moose antler."

operose [OP-er-owss] (adjective)

Industrious; diligent

"Before his morning coffee, Winston was comatose; afterward, he was **operose**."

opuscule [oh-PUSS-kyool] (noun)

A small, minor work

"For this we appeal to Newton's *Principia*, or to Euler's ***Opuscule***, where he gives a very beautiful investigation of the velocity of the aerial pulses...."
—"Pneumatics" in *The New and Complete American Encyclopedia* (1810)

"**Opuscule**"—it sounds like a fancy word for a pimple, doesn't it? The **opuscule** I'm working on at the moment (though only in my head so far) is a short fictional story about a woman plagued by a squeaky shoe. There are certain sounds that I find intensely annoying, and that is one of them. Others are the classic nails on a chalkboard, audio feedback, balloon rubbing, nose blowing, and smoke-detector bleeping. Put me in a room with all of those sounds occurring at once—no **opuscule** that—and I think my head would explode.

orc [ork] (noun)

A mythical creature, a monster, demon, goblin, etc.

"Art thou not **Orc**, who serpent-form'd
Stands at the gate of Enitharmon to devour her children?
Blasphemous Demon, Antichrist, hater of Dignities,
Lover of wild rebellion, and transgressor of God's Law,
Why dost thou come to Angel's eyes in this terrific form?"
—William Blake, *America: A Prophecy* (1793)

This word occurs most often in fantasy literature, most notably in Tolkien's works. The **orc** around where I live would be the Jersey Devil, a creature most often described as being similar to a pterosaur. It is said to live in the New Jersey Pine Barrens and seems to inspire as much affection as fear. There's even a hockey team named after it.

ordalian [or-DA-li-an] (adjective)

Relating to an ordeal

"Owing to his 'delicate' back, Zachary considered any task requiring physical labor to be an **ordalian** imposition."

oscitancy [OSS-it-an-see] (noun)

1. The act of yawning
2. The state of being drowsy or inattentive; dullness

"Melanie began to describe her shopping trip, but Nick couldn't hide his **oscitancy**."

oscitate [OSS-it-ayt] (verb)

To yawn or gape

"There are persons whose physical constitutions are so delicate that mere thoughts of taking snuff (and medicines generally) produce the same effect as inhaling the powder itself: now, if the imagination of the reader has a similar influence over his system, he can have no disposition to **oscitate** while finishing the chapter; on the contrary, the greatest obstacle to his progress will arise from a disposition to sneeze."
—Thomas Ewbank, *The Spoon* (1844)

Perhaps you felt an uncontrollable desire to **oscitate** while reading the above. Believe me, that's the most entertaining use of the word I could find, and one of the few I could find outside of a dictionary.

I remember a rather traumatic experience I had with **oscitation** when I was in third grade. We used to have reading circle, during which the teacher would sit with seven or eight students while we took turns reading aloud. The book we were reading that day was a dull one, and I kept stifling a yawn. The teacher noticed this, and after the fifth or sixth stifle, she reached over, grabbed my nose and my chin, and forced my mouth open. "Now, yawn!" she commanded. The other kids thought this was hilarious. To this day, I feel embarrassed whenever I **oscitate** in public. That teacher might be suspended for doing that today.

ostrobogulous [os-tro-BOG-yoo-luss](adjective)

Something weird, bizarre, unusual or pornographic

"Mother doesn't want to go to the movies. She calls them agglomerations of **ostrobogulous** fantasies."

I'm going to try to use this word at Thanksgiving dinner sometime. There's a certain **ostrobogulous** casserole dish my mom makes that may provide the opportunity.

P

palter [POL-ter] (verb)

To talk or act insincerely, use trickery or equivocate

"He had faked illnesses before, so I couldn't tell whether he was **paltering** or faltering."

pandiculate [pan-dik-yuh-LAYT] (verb) **pandiculation** (noun)

To stretch and yawn simultaneously

"I'm troubled with **pandiculation**,
An ailment dire and rooted deep
'Tis caused by undue hesitation
In rising from the couch of sleep."
—George W. E. Daniels, "Pandiculation," in *The Medical Pickwick* (1921)

I **pandiculate**, you **pandiculate**, we all **pandiculate**. I try to avoid doing it at work, or in awkward situations—like when someone thinks he/she is relating a fascinating narrative full of riveting details. Or when watching one of the cable movies on the Lifetime channel that a significant other invites onto our TV screen.

panjandrum [pan-JAN-drum] (noun)

An important person, a VIP—or someone who thinks he or she is (sometimes capitalized)

"Lucy said, that if it had not been for the grand **Panjandrum**, she was almost sure she should have been able to say it; but she was so much surprised by meeting the grand **Panjandrum** himself again, and so diverted by the little round button at top, that she could think of nothing else...."
—Maria Edgeworth, "Miss Edgeworth's Harry and Lucy," in *The London Magazine* (1826)

"**Panjandrum**" is sometimes used as a metaphorical synonym for other things, such as an explosive weapon used by the British military in World War II, and even for the Supreme Being. (I prefer to refer to the latter as The Cosmic Muffin.)

pareidolia [par-eye-DOE-li-uh] (noun)

An imagined perception of a pattern or meaning where none exists

"… [the] objective stimulus blends with the deficient subjective stimulus, and forms a single complete impression. This last is called by Dr. Kahlbaum, changing hallucination, partial hallucination, perception of secondary images, or **pareidolia**."
—John Sibbald, M.D., "German Psychological Literature," in *The Journal of Mental Science* (1868)

When I was a kid I was "imaginative" and used to see miniature worlds in wallpaper patterns, faces in wood grain and cloud banks, and a demon's head and shoulders in a painting my grandmother had of Washington State's Snoqaulmie Falls. I lost my **pareidolia** as I grew up, though I still occasionally see things that aren't there out of the corner of my eye. Lately, it's been mice in moving shadows. Except sometimes it really *is* mice.

pasticcio [pa-STEE-cho] (noun)

A work or style consisting of borrowed fragments, ingredients, or motifs assembled from various sources; a potpourri

"What did it matter if the work were a spurious thing, a **pasticcio**, a poor victim which had been pulled this way and that, changed, cut, added to?"
—Robert Smythe Hichens, *The Way of Ambition* (1913)

"On one occasion an old man sang quite glibly a tune which was in reality a **pasticcio** of three separate shanties all known to me."
—Sir Richard Runciman Terry, *The Shanty Book*, Sailor Shanties (1921)

Hey, all you word aficionados, I know this sounds like something you might order in an Italian restaurant, but it appears in the *American Heritage Dictionary of the English Language*. A book I read (or, perhaps you might call it a monograph), entitled *Old World Politics, New World Prophecy*, is billed as an explanation of *Inland Empire*, the very confusing but weirdly fascinating (to me anyway) film by David Lynch, which is sort of a cinematic **pasticcio**. The author delves into Eastern European mythology and other arcana to develop a theory of what the film is about, and he even argues that the talking-rabbit sitcom scenes (yes, *Inland Empire* is that strange) were not non sequiturs. (If something is not a non, is it a plain old sequitur?) The book, itself a bit of a **pasticcio**, received excellent reviews from Lynch fans.

peccant [PEK-unt] (adjective)

Offensive, guilty, unprincipled

"'There you have it. Make the most of it. Your frock's too filthy, but I came to sacrifice myself.' Maisie looked at the **peccant** places; there were moments when it was a relief to her to drop her eyes even on something so sordid."
—Henry James, *What Maisie Knew* (1897)

Why do I find this humorous? Getting so bent out of shape over some spots on someone's "frock" is over-the-top enough to make me giggle, at least in the context of over-the-top belletrist Henry James, with his endless dependent clauses. The uncharacteristically curt and **peccant** quote above presses my literary absurdity button.

pecksniffian [pek-SNIFF-ee-an] (adjective)

Pretending to be benevolent or to have high moral principles, like the Charles Dickens character Mr. Pecksniff

"There is something quite pestilently **Pecksniffian** about shrinking from a hard task on the plea that it is not hard enough. If a man will really try talking to the ten beggars who come to his door he will soon find out whether it is really so much easier than…writing a cheque for a hospital."
—G.K. Chesterton, *What's Wrong with the World* (1912)

I live in a city with a large population of Jehovah's Witnesses. These are religious fanatics who believe the end of the world is near and publish a free magazine on the subject, *The Watchtower*, which they keep trying to give away. They're always standing around at the local train station, dressed like they're going to Sunday chapel and smiling enigmatically. I often pass them on the street, too, and they'll invariably say, very politely, "Something to read this morning, sir?" as they hold out their rag. "No thank you," I say. "Have a nice day," they say in a **pecksniffian** way. I know what they're thinking: "You'll burn in eternal hell fire, you damn foolish sinner."

pellucid [puh-LOO-sid] (adjective)

Transparent or translucent, extremely clear

"Any writer who has read even a little will know what is meant by the word intelligible. It is not sufficient that there be a meaning that may be hammered out of the sentence, but that the language should be so **pellucid** that the meaning should be rendered without an effort of the reader—and not only some proposition of meaning, but the very sense, no more and no less, which the writer has intended to put into his words."
—Anthony Trollope, *An Autobiography* (1883)

The **pellucid** water of my aquarium isn't so pellucid at the moment. How can a few tiny zebra fish and some miniscule neon tetras create such murk? Time to change the filter. And maybe feed them less. If I was a fish, I wouldn't want to live in dirty water. After all, *a fish can't take a bath*. That's my ecological slogan. I should put it on a button or a tee shirt.

penetralia [pen-eh-TRAY-lee-uh] (noun)

The innermost parts of a structure, especially a temple sanctuary; the most private or secret part of something

"'True,' answered my wife. "And in that sense we are a mystery to our neighbors.'
'Doubtless we are,' said I. 'Doubtless there have been questions asked about us many times which none answered satisfactorily, and which still remain as unsolved problems. There is a **penetralia** in every family.'"
—Timothy Shay Arthur, *Our Neighbors in the Corner House* (1866)

I wish my neighbors *were* more of a mystery. On a typical weekend we might be treated to both their barking dog, who glares down at us from their elevated back deck as we putter around in the backyard, and a loud 1950s rock-and-roll concert from their **penetralia** via their open windows.

peregrinate [PER-i-gruh-nayt] (verb)

To journey or travel from place to place

"I wish I could **peregrinate** around the universe," said Will, "and still sleep in my own bed."

perspicacious [per-spih-CAY-shus] (adjective) **perspicacity** (noun)

Having keen understanding, mental perception or discernment

"You are **perspicacious**, know the ways of the world, and are more tactful than most men of your age. Do you think the count is really what he appears to be?"
—Alexandre Dumas, *The Count of Monte Cristo* (1846)

Sometimes I think I'm good at seeing through people—at **perspicacity** [per-spih-CA-sity]—but then I find out they have as many layers as an onion, and I've only penetrated the skin at the top. You find out the quiet guy is writing horror scripts in his spare time. The corporate executive is teaching guitar lessons on the side. And the checkout lady of a certain age at the supermarket wows everybody with a jaw-dropping dance routine on *American Idol.* (All true.) It's a good thing I like people who are full of surprises. Otherwise, I would spend a lot of time being disconcerted.

perspicuous [per-SPIK-yoo-us] (adjective)

Easily understood, clear

"Though expressing the lofty thoughts, and exhibiting the subtle coarse of reasoning suggested in their own minds, those who write upon such subjects, may be **perspicuous**, and yet far from 'universally intelligible.'"
—W. F. P., "Dr. Channing and Lord Brougham," quoted in *The Southern*

Literary Messenger (1840)

One of my favorite TV shows was *L O S T*, about a group of plane-crash survivors on a tropical island. Or was it? What this alternate-reality series was really about is far from **perspicuous**, but that was the secret of its appeal, I think.

pertinacious [per-tin-AY-shus] (adjective)

Stubborn or persistent

"And those, indeed, who have certain opinions of their own, are **pertinacious** through pleasure and pain. For they rejoice when they are victorious, if they are not induced to change their opinion, and they are grieved when their opinions, as if they were decrees, are without efficacy."
—Aristotle, *Nicomachean Ethics* (Thomas Taylor, translator, 1818)

"He behaved like some tricksy elf, uttering his most **pertinacious** screeches in time of family prayer, and distorting his visage at poor Mr. Little into such curiously ugly shapes as daunted the feeble divine from any caressing approaches whatever."
—Rose Terry Cooke, "Aceldama Sparks" (1886)

I am **pertinacious** in my determination to...what? Not a lot I can think of. To correct grammar and infelicities of expression, I suppose, but that's part of my job. There are the usual things that most everyone is persistent about, like brushing my teeth. I eat the same thing for breakfast every day, but that's more about being a creature of habit than "stubborn." I've known **pertinacious** people in my time, though, who shall be nameless, because they could very well be reading this. Some of the most interesting, otherwise likable people I've met are **pertinacious** about the most ridiculous things—like not ever getting on an airplane or neglecting to see a doctor or just refusing to compromise with the nexus of imbroglios we call life in the 21st century. Yes, stupidly stubborn and unwilling to compromise. Maybe they should run for Congress?

petrichor [PET-rik-ur] (noun)

The pleasant smell of rain on dry ground; the yellow organic oil that yields this scent

"Millicent opened the window as the rain clouds dispersed and breathed deeply the **petrichor** that wafted in."

There's not much **petrichor** around here as I write this, since there's not any dry ground. Instead, there's more of a wet pavement smell. Rain, rain, go away.

pettifogger [PET-ee-fog-ger] (noun)

A petty, quibbling, unscrupulous lawyer

"Football hero to B-movie actor to homicidal maniac to full-time duffer: a phalanx of **pettifoggers** ensured his acquittal."

philocomal [FI-lo-cohm-al] (adjective)

Characterized by excessive concern with one's hair

"There were ladies present too; and after some pleasant little discourse, all tending to the glorification of hair-dressing, an eminent professor of the **philocomal** art there present proceeded to a series of practical and illustrative experiments on the heads of some of the young ladies...."
—George Augustus Sala, *Twice 'Round the Clock* (1858)

One summer I got my hair cut—and cut and cut. My (ahem) stylist decided that, since "it's summer now," I needed a short cut. I agreed, thinking he meant "a little shorter than usual." Instead, I got shorn like a sheep. I almost looked like I was ready for boot camp. I became obsessed with **philocomal** mirror gazing and even went out and bought a fedora. But the haircut grew on me—literally and figuratively. It looked pretty terrific within a couple of weeks—or three.

pilgarlic [pil-GAR-lik] (noun)

A bald head; someone regarded with slight or mock pity

"'I'm not going to scold, and you know it,' he answered quietly. 'I thought you had made up your mind to remain at home, for once. Now comes this new **pilgarlic** and orders you off again to Florida. On what excuse?'"
—Philip Verrill Mighels, *The Pillars of Eden* (1909)

I saw a bald-headed, couture-clad woman walking on Fifth Avenue one day. Typically for New York City, no one seemed to take much notice. (I did, but I'm an enthusiastic people-watcher.) You have to wonder what the motivation is for a seemingly healthy young woman to shave her head. Men, natural **pilgarlics**, often go to great lengths, and great expense, to avoid the chrome-dome look. And women spend huge amounts of time and money on their manes.

According to a blog I read after performing a Google search related to this quandary, the best reason for a woman to shave her head is "to prove that she is beautiful." So, no more distracting locks taking attention away from a pretty face—and no more hiding a plain one behind a gorgeous mop. It's brave and honest, I guess. But somehow I don't think the Rogaine company has anything to worry about.

pinchbeck [PINCH-bek] (noun or adjective)

Something cheap or counterfeit; an alloy used to imitate gold

"Magdalen was counting on the sale of Aunt Philomena's wedding band to finance her trip to the Azores. It was Mr. Dash's sad duty to inform her that it was nothing but a **pinchbeck** curtain ring."

piste [peest] (noun)

A ski trail; a beaten track or trail

"He then delivered some poetic utterances about the snow-covered hills visible through another window, which led to some reflections on the pleasures of cross-country skiing off the regular **piste**."

When I was growing up in the wilds of upstate New York, there was a wooded area and a river behind my house. Through the woods along the river was a narrow trail, about a foot and a half wide and a half-mile long, with dense foliage on either side. People—kids and teenagers—used this foot path to go from the town park to a certain point in the river where they used to skinny-dip or fish. I don't think any of this happens anymore, and I suspect the "**piste**" has disappeared by now. (I should find out the next time I visit my hometown.) As a kid I used to have dreams about this trail, nightmares sometimes, about walking along it at night or being chased by someone—or some *thing*. I think I still do, but I don't often remember dreams anymore.

It's strange the byways of memory that stumbling across a certain word or phrase will take you down.

poltroon [pol-TROON] (noun)

A coward

"Every educated man of the nineteenth century is, and must always be, a **poltroon** and a slave; it is his normal condition."
—Fyodor Dostoyevsky, *Letters from the Underworld* (1864)

My normal condition, as an educated man of the twenty-first century, is as a fragmented simulacrum of a purveyor of pastiche. So say the post-modernists, anyway. Perhaps Dostoyevsky would simply say "**poltroon!**"

pooka [POO-kuh](noun)

A mischievous spirit or trickster (derived from Irish folklore)

"The moment he came in sight the **Pooka** changed himself into a squirrel and ran up the oak tree; Angus changed himself into a turnip and lay at the Dagda's feet...."
—Ella Young, *Celtic Wonder-Tales* (1910)

So it's a "**pooka**" who's always hiding the remote control? Hmm. There *are* a lot of mischievous squirrels in my yard. Not too many mysterious turnips, though.

pooterish [POO-ter-ish] (adjective)

Pompous, self-important, bourgeois

"A bowler hat would be rather **pooterish** attire for your garden-variety gnome, don't you think?"

"**Pooterish**" comes from Charles Pooter, the hero of a 19th-century novel called *Diary of a Nobody*. (Yes, I'm thinking of adding that to my list of potential new titles for my blog.)

popinjay [POP-in-jay] (noun)

A vain or conceited person

"When Victoria discovered that Friedrich had a whole album of photographic self portraits, she began to think of him as a bit of a **popinjay**."

postiche [poss-TEESH] (adjective)

Added superfluously or inappropriately; artificial

"To his mind, a **postiche** portico made Herbert's cottage a mansion."

potvaliant [POT-veyl-yunt] (adjective)

Brave because drunk

"'I was **potvaliant**,' Aiden said, by way of explaining his uncharacteristic foray into fire-walking."

preterist [PRET-er-ist] (noun)

1. Someone who is only or mostly interested in the past
2. In theology, someone who thinks the prophecies in the Book of Revelation have already been fulfilled or nearly so

"The **preterist** holds that the book refers to events that are now long past. These are the triumphs of Christianity over Judaism and Paganism, resulting

in the fall of Jerusalem and of pagan Rome."
—J. G. Murphy, *The Book of Revelation; or The Last Volume of Prophecy* (1882)

I think I'm a **preterist**, but I haven't read the Book of Revelation in a long time. I remember it as being like something you'd dream after eating bad clams and falling asleep in a sauna.

pridian [PRID-ee-an] (adjective)

Relating to yesterday

"Thrice a-week, at least, does Gann breakfast in bed—sure sign of **pridian** intoxication."
—William Makepeace Thackeray, *A Shabby Genteel Story* (1857)

What's for dinner? I've often noticed that **pridian** leftovers, when reheated, taste better the second time around.

propinquitous [proh-PING-kwi-tuss] (adjective)

Near in time or place; close to

"Was Lillie to be married to young Whitewood, or some other conveniently **propinquitous** admirer?"
—John W. De Forest, *Miss Ravenel's Conversion* (1867)

The questions I ask myself every time November rolls around: "Halloween has come and gone already? The holidays are **propinquitous**? Where's the pause button?"

prosopopoeia [pro-so-puh-PEE-uh] (noun)

Personification; speaking in the voice of an absent or imaginary person, or an inanimate object

"The **prosopopoeia** of Solomon is in the midst of other passages of a like kind; and there is no part of it inconsistent with those rules which are not of modern invention, but are essential to the nature and the beauty of this figure."

—George Hill, *Lectures in Divinity* (1833)

Here's my attempt at poetic **prosopopoeia**:

Camera

My cool eye never lies; it only leaves things out.
I will freeze and preserve whatever you show me,
untainted by brushstrokes or bias.

And my memory is infinite, though fixed in a square.

People must like me; they smile and smile,
though I sometimes record what they don't want to see:
wattles and wrinkles, wars and atrocities.

I can even retain the faces of the dead—
all glossy and flat and just out of reach.

The sad ones revere my rectangular moments.
They search the trapped shadows
for what really happened or what they want to believe.
But I only offer a world of dots,
suspect emotions caught in a flash,
and no amount of staring can bring back a day or a wife.

Still, everyone keeps me pointing and clicking,
trying to catch the Grand Canyon, perhaps,
or a baby's smile before it fades, birthday by birthday,
into an old man's grimace in a silver frame.

puissance [PYOO-ih-sunss] (noun)

Ability to influence or coerce; having a controlling influence

"Where is the graveyard of dead gods? What lingering mourner waters their
mounds? There was a time when Jupiter was the king of the gods, and any
man who doubted his **puissance** was ipso facto a barbarian and an

ignoramus. But where in all the world is there a man who worships Jupiter today?"
—H. L. Mencken, "Where is the graveyard of dead gods?" in *The Smart Set* (1922)

He may not have **puissance** anymore, but Jupiter did have a humongous blob of methane gas in space named after him. That's some consolation, I think.

punctiform [PUNK-tuh-form] (adjective)

Shaped or formed like a point or dot

"Each of his ideas would vanish in the act of awakening its successor; his mind (if such it could be called) would be shut up to the **punctiform** instant; he would obey, without noticing, the current which swept him on; drift to his conclusions, but never know why...."
—William James, M.D., "The Association of Ideas," in *Popular Science* (1880)

A strange word, which yields a number of weird, rather icky (though safe for work) images if you search for it on Google Images.

A short story by Italo Calvino in his book *Cosmicomics* must hold the world record for the number of uses of "**punctiform**" in a sentence. The circa 1965 short story is narrated by an entity existing inside the conceptual point that contained all matter before the Big Bang, before time and space existed. (We would call it a singularity today.) That's a "state," if you will, that the human mind can't conceive of, but Calvino, by giving it a humorous voice, makes it a somewhat approachable notion.

pyknic [PIK-nik] (adjective)

Short, stocky, endomorphic (fat)

"'If you don't stop feeding table scraps to that dog,' she warned, 'you'll soon have a **pyknic** Pekingese.'"

Q

quidam [QUID-ahm] (noun)

A someone; a person unknown

"A **quidam** called me this afternoon, but it was a wrong number. 'No one here by that name,' I informed the caller, who was very apologetic before hanging up. I'm always tempted to play along when this sort of thing happens."

New-age gymnastic troupe and spectacle purveyor Cirque du Soleil mounted a show called ***Quidam***. They define the word as "...a nameless passer-by, a solitary figure lingering on a street corner, a person rushing past.... One who cries out, sings and dreams within us all."

The **quidams** I encounter every day are a lot less phantasmagoric. I see the same people daily during my work commute, but I have no idea who they are. There's the Hassid, the weirdo, the suburban soccer-mom in training, the librarian, etc. At least that's how I think of them, based on whatever visual stereotype they conform to. I see these people more often than members of my extended family, but I don't know their names. I've never spoken to them. There's a recognition, though—something fleeting in the eyes when we see each other. We'll never speak unless the train breaks down, I suppose. Sometimes I fantasize about inviting them all to a party, though: RSVP.

quidnunc [KWID-nunk] (noun)

A nosy person; busybody

"'Close the blinds,' Mildred commanded. 'Do you want every passing **quidnunc** to know you're a beer-swilling couch tuber?'"

A guy at work brews and bottles his own beer in his basement, and he gave me some one day to try—a dark stout. Not bad, though it lacked fizz. I thought he should create his own brand and label. (He uses recycled beer bottles and keeps the original labels.) Something like "Kelt & Kraut" beer—he's Irish and German and uses that as his online name. But it's up to him. I don't want to be a **quidnunc**.

quinate [QWEYE-nate] (adjective)

Arranged or appearing in groups of five

"She removed her spike-heeled shoe, revealing her one deformity: her toes were not **quinate**. Indeed, she had six toes on her left foot, immaculately pedicured, and with each nail painted a different color, so that the effect was like a six-hued rainbow. She caught me staring at this polydactyl anomaly. 'Just a little more of me to love,' she said."

Marilyn Monroe was rumored to have six toes on one foot, but that is a myth. She had "something extra," but it wasn't a toe.

Polydactylism (having one or more extra fingers or toes) occurs fairly frequently in cats, and Ernest Hemingway, among his many other quirks, loved six-toed felines. According to Wikipedia, when Hemingway died in 1961, his house in Key West, Florida, became a museum and a home for his many cats, "and it currently houses approximately fifty descendants of his cats (about half of which are polydactyl)."

Often I wish my fingers were more than **quinate** when I'm typing. Those Z and Q keys are a stretch. Don't get me started on "qwerty."

quodlibet [KWOD-luh-bet] (noun)

A piece of music combining several different melodies in a humorous way

"Alex was whistling to pass the time, but the tune changed every five seconds, until he ran out of repertoire.
'Don't stop! I love **quodlibet**,' said Alicia.
'That wasn't it; I don't know that one,' said Alex. 'Hum a few bars?'"

quondam [KWON-dum] (adjective)

That once was; former

"The **quondam** addict was now perfectly abstemious."

R

rampageous [ram-PEY-juss] (adjective)

Raging, frenzied

"That's the very thing, sir; which they're all talkin' about it at the house, sir, and how a poor invalid gentleman, what could scarce stir hand or foot, should get up in the middle of the night and saddle his own horse and ride away at a **rampageous** rate...."
—Mary Elizabeth Braddon, *Henry Dunbar* (1864)

Knowing the definition, would you ever name your cat or your charter boat "**Rampageous**"? Google says you might.

rannygazoo [ran-ee-ga-ZOO] (noun)

A joke or prank

"Bob couldn't think of a proper **rannygazoo**, but then, in an idle moment it came to him: he would serve Tom a peanut butter and tuna fish sandwich."

An idle moment. It seems people either don't have enough of those these days, or they have far too many. And when you have too much time on your hands, well, you may start planning a few too many **rannygazoos**.

rantipole [RAN-ti-pohl] (noun, adjective or verb)

A wild, reckless person

"This **rantipole** hero had for some time singled out the blooming Katrina for the object of his uncouth gallantries, and though his amorous toyings were something like the gentle caresses and endearments of a bear, yet it was whispered that she did not altogether discourage his hopes."
—Washington Irving, "The Legend of Sleepy Hollow" (1820)

In the Bizarro universe, I suppose I would be a **rantipole**. As it is, I'm the opposite of wild and crazy, at least in my outward behavior. My interior life is a bit more rambunctious. About the wildest thing I do (and I don't do it often) is to scream into a pillow when feeling especially frustrated. I recommend it. It's quite cathartic and doesn't alarm the neighbors. A few decades ago, there was even a psychotherapy technique built around screaming, called Primal therapy. (There was a popular book about it, *The Primal Scream.*) John and Yoko took it up, and the result was a great easy-listenin' album (I jest) called *Plastic Ono Band.* You don't hear much about Primal screaming these days, though, and it's too bad, because the world has plenty to scream about. Grab a pillow, I say.

ratiocination [RASH-ee-oss-in-AY-tion] (noun)

The process of exact thinking or a reasoned train of thought

"The **ratiocination** actually passing through the mind in the solution of even a single cryptograph, if detailed step by step, would fill a large volume."
—Edgar Allan Poe, "A Few Words on Secret Writing," in *Graham's Magazine* (1841)

Ratiocination is an important concept in mystery stories, of course, from Poe's day to the present. I'm not a big fan of formulaic mystery stories, in which the author creates a stupid character who says "What?" simply to allow the protagonist to explain some obscure concept. These Dr. Watson characters are stand-ins for the reader, of course. I suppose they're a necessary evil, so the reader can follow the detective's **ratiocination**.

rebarbative [ree-BAR-buh-tiv] (adjective)

Tending to irritate or repel

"[T]hey read Modern History not because they have any vocation for its study, or any special interest in it, but simply and solely because their college compels them to offer some Honour School, and they hope to find this one rather less **rebarbative** than Law or Mathematics, Theology or Physical Science."

—Charles Oman, "Inaugural Lecture on the Study of History" (1906)

The world is full of **rebarbative** people, many of whom insist on riding the PATH commuter train between Newark, New Jersey, and Manhattan at rush hour, like the guy who asked me if the train was going to New York. When I said yes, he asked two other people the same question—as if it was a matter of opinion and he needed to take a survey.

rebus [REE-bus] (noun)

A representation of a word or phrase by pictures or symbols

"A century or two ago the science of **rebuses** and devices was much studied and in vogue; but they are now out of date, and we laugh at such conceits.... I have heard of a rebus for Babington; a baby issuing out of a tun [i.e., a large cask]."
—*The Gentleman's Magazine* (1789)

Of course the ancient Egyptians, with their hieroglyphics, were the most famous users of the **rebus**. I'm guessing our desktop and smartphone icons would seem far more puzzling to Gutenberg than to Tutankhamen.

relume [rih-LOOM] (verb)

To make bright or clear again; illuminate again

"'Open the blinds and **relume** this domicile,' the pretentious Mr. Wexfordcromby commanded. 'It might help if you removed your sunglasses,' Millicent retorted."

resile [ri-ZILE] (verb)

To bounce or spring back, to draw back, to recoil

"The envelope that Sheila had left so perilously close to the stovetop ignited, and instantly her hand **resiled** from the fire."

The inner mind is like an autopilot, I suppose. It's the part of your mind that can, for example, continue to drive a car while your conscious thoughts are a dozen light years away from the road. Or, while you're out for your morning constitutional, **resile** from dog droppings on the sidewalk while mentally reviewing your to-do list. I write from experience.

revenant [REV-uh-nahnt] (noun)

One who returns from a long absence or from death

"'Since when has this **revenant** taken to appear?' inquired George North, after a short period of reflection. 'Since Anthony's disappearance?'

'Oh, for a long, long while before it. I believe the monk died something like two hundred years ago. Why? Were you thinking, George, that it might be the **revenant** of poor Anthony?'"
—Ellen Wood, *The Master of Greylands* (1874)

Hamlet saw his dead father, or did he? Soon after my own father died, I also saw (thought I saw?) his **revenant**, driving a pick-up truck—something my father, more of a guy's guy than I am, enjoyed doing. This specter, or perhaps this fellow who *strongly* resembled my father, had a big grin on his face as he sped down the highway. I felt a little better about my dad's death after that.

rhathymia [ruh-THY-mia] (noun)

Light-hearted, carefree behavior

"The Beatles proved that one could combine **rhathymia** with mayhem in 'Maxwell's Silver Hammer,' their bizarrely jaunty little ditty about a serial killer."

I need more **rhathymia**. Maybe we all do. When I first encountered this word, it occurred to me that the last time I had engaged in any **rhathymia** was during the local Artist's Studio Tour, when I visited the studio of a sculptor who makes large Rube Goldberg-style contraptions out of metal pipes, wooden sticks, gears, bicycle chains, small electric motors, and dripping water. Many of them included hand cranks that visitors could turn to make various gadgets perform actions, like opening and closing a fish mouth (some of them were in the form of metallic fish) or make water tip cups over and ring bells. As I turned those cranks, I was five years old again... except...I kept thinking about the word **rhathymia**.

rixatrix [RIKS-a-triks] (noun)

A quarrelsome, scolding woman; a bitch

"As for Mrs. Hotchkick, there is some evidence of design in her creation, for, **rixatrix** that she was, she seemed to have been made on purpose for Hotchkick."
—August Berkeley, *A Modern Quixote, or My Wife's Fool of a Husband* (1884)

A **rixatrix** may be tough to deal with in real life (and I've met a few), but they do make for compelling characters in film and literature. Just think about *The Taming of the Shrew*, an entire play built around a verbal blitzkrieg between a loquacious bitch and a multiloquent.... (What is the male equivalent of a bitch? A bastard?)

In Edward Albee's *Who's Afraid of Virginia Woolf*, one of my favorite plays (and also an excellent Richard Burton/Elizabeth Taylor movie), the two main characters, George and Martha, have a *Taming of the Shrew*-type verbal battle that's as thrilling as Shakespeare's—or more so, now, since the cruise missiles fly in the modern vernacular. I even wrote a paper about the play in college. Or a few papers, if I recall. It can be analyzed from several thematic angles: Freudian, rhetorical, dramatic, even political: George and Martha, hmm.

Tell the scold in your life (male or female) to "stop being such a **rixatrix**," and see what kind of reaction you get. My guess is that it will stop the castigation cold—at least until he or she finds a dictionary.

rodomontade [rod-uh-mon-TADE (-TAHD)] (noun)

Bragging or bluster, or a rant

"I put down the phone long before Ronald finished his **rodomontade**."

roun [rown] (noun or verb)

A whisper, or to whisper
"Another **rouned** to his fellow low."

—Chaucer, "The Squire's Tale," *The Canterbury Tales* (1380s?)

An obsolete word, replaced by "whisper." Why do words fall out of favor? In this case, maybe because "whisper," with its *S* sound, actually *sounds* more like a whisper.

I remember a game we used to play as kids: tell a friend you have a secret and then just make a *pssst pssst* **roun** in his or her ear, making the friend giggle and driving the other kids crazy. ("What is it? What is it?")

rowel [RAO-el] (noun) **rowelled** (adjective)

A small wheel with star-like points at the end of a cowboy's spur

"In the reign of Henry III, the **rowelled** spur made its first appearance; the **rowel** was gradually lengthened till it reached its maximum of seven inches and a half, in the time of Henry VI."
—Robert Chambers, *The Book of Days* (1832)

I've only ridden a horse twice, but I didn't wear **rowels**! It was an odd feeling being on top of a swaying animal (although not as weird—or as swaying—as the time I rode an elephant). I don't know what to compare it to. The horse was hard to steer I remember. It was sort of like driving a car that doesn't have power steering. I began to understand exactly why **rowels** exist.

runcible [RUNSS-ih-bul] (adjective)

A nonsense word with no particular meaning; sometimes referring to a spoon with fork tines

"'Dear pig, are you willing to sell for one shilling
Your ring?' Said the Piggy, 'I will.'
So they took it away, and were married next day
By the Turkey who lives on the hill.
They dined on mince, and slices of quince,
Which they ate with a **runcible** spoon;
And hand in hand, on the edge of the sand,
They danced by the light of the moon,

The moon,
The moon,
They danced by the light of the moon."
—Edward Lear, "The Owl and the Pussycat" (1871)

Since this word, invented by Lear, has no precise or standard original meaning (though spoon manufacturers have glommed onto it), we can, I think, use it to mean whatever we want it to mean. (Isn't it interesting that the word "mean" can mean both "malicious" and "what you have in mind"? This indicates a jaundiced attitude toward human nature, I think.)

~~~I have a **runcible** mannequin sitting in an antique wheelchair in my living room.
~~~I'm dreaming of a **runcible** Christmas
~~~I have 215 **runcible** friends on the Book of Faces.
~~~The tofu burger I had last night was **runcible** indeed.
~~~Is *Eraserhead, Fire Walk With Me,* or *Inland Empire* the most **runcible** David Lynch film?
~~~"I Want You (She's So **Runcible**)"
~~~I drink my coffee **runcible**.

Let's all try to slip this word into conversation and see what kinds of reactions we get.

rusticate [RUHS-ti-kayt] (verb)

To go to or live in the country; to send to the country

"'Live in the city and **rusticate** on weekends?' said Malcolm. 'How bourgeois.'"

rutilant [ROOT-ih-lunt] (adjective)

Bright red in color

"Though Prudence pretended to be unaffected by off-color jokes, her **rutilant** face gave her away."

S

sabermetrician [SAY-ber-meh-TRISH-uhn] (noun)

Someone who studies baseball statistics

"Ambrose—always reluctant to admit to his opulent life of uninterrupted leisure—hesitated over the survey form. At last, with a sardonic smile, he filled in his occupation as '**sabermetrician**.'"

saccade [sa-KAHD] (noun)

A small, rapid movement of the eye

"Watching Henry as he turned the pages of *Gravity's Rainbow*, I was fascinated by the **saccades** of his left eye, which seemed to oscillate faster than his right."

I've never been able to plow my way through a Thomas Pynchon mega-novel like *Gravity's Rainbow*, sad to say, despite my determined **saccades**. I've been trying to read his novel *V* for years. I have read the slender *The Crying of Lot 49* and liked it, though. Where are the *Reader's Digest* condensed editions when you need them?

salmagundi [sal-muh-GUN-dee] (noun)

A mixture or assortment; a medley; a potpourri; a miscellany

"Clive, an inveterate packrat, lived amidst a heaping **salmagundi** of inutile junk."

salubrious [sah-LOO-bree-us] (adjective)

Healthful

"We have the unqualified testimony of the most distinguished philosophers

and medical authors of ancient and modern times, that water is the most **salubrious** drink of which we have any knowledge."
—Sylvester Graham, *A Defence of the Graham System of Living* (1835)

I'm convinced that drinking coffee is **salubrious**, despite what anyone says. It doesn't have as many antioxidants as green tea, but it does have some. And it has water in it! How can it not be **salubrious**?

sardoodledum [sar-DOO-duhl-duhm] (noun)

Dramatic works with exaggerated, contrived, trivial, or deplorable plots; soap opera; melodrama

"As for Sudermann, he chose to temper the rigors of the Schalf-Holz formula (by Ibsen out of Zola) with **sardoodledum**. The result was this 'Heimat,' in which naturalism was wedded to a mellow sentimentality, caressing to audiences bred upon the drama of perfumed adultery."
—H. L. Mencken, "Hermann Sudermann," in *Prejudices: First Series* (1919)

Sometimes life imitates daytime drama. A Christmas party I attended a few years ago was given by a woman who was widowed, then decided to have a child with a married man who moved to Germany, but whom she managed to visit there periodically, along with their two-year-old son.

Meanwhile, as she was planning this party (with a very animated two-year-old "monkey" underfoot), her father lay dying in the hospital, and she was expecting a number of relatives from elsewhere around the nation to arrive within a day or so (to say their farewells to Father); they would all be staying in her tiny condominium. Also meanwhile, she had been constructing a labyrinthine website showcase for her paintings.

I was mightily impressed. Under similar circumstances, I can't imagine summoning the enterprise to mount a Christmas party (or even to get out of bed), but some people manage to survive and even thrive while living in a melodrama, a soap opera, a true-life **sardoodledum**.

By the way, when you search for "**sardoodledum**" in Google Images, for some reason, many depictions of the Beatles, and specifically the "cute one," result. Ob-la-di, ob-la-da.

sarnie [SAR-nee] (noun)

A sandwich (chiefly British)

"'Make me an egg and bacon **sarnie**, will you?'Lionel said. 'Oh, make it yourself,' replied Jean."

When we (the wife and I) had "high tea" at the British Museum during our visit to London, they served us **sarnies**—little finger sandwiches with the crusts cut off. Watercress or something. So *twee*. Then they served us tea from tea *bags*, which I thought was a bit odd, given that everything else about the menu and setting was posh. But what do I know? Maybe Her Majesty the Queen dunks a bag in her cup these days. The quality of tea time is not strained....

scandent [SKAN-dent] (adjective)

Botany; meaning climbing, as with a vine

"**Scandent** tendrils of ivy seemed to have consumed the old house."

scapegrace [SKAYP-grayse] (noun)

A mischief maker, a scoundrel

"Alaeddin continued in his former ill courses and, when his mother saw that her spouse had deceased, and that her son was a **scapegrace** and good for nothing at all, she sold the shop and what so was to be found therein and fell to spinning cotton yarn."
—Sir Richard Burton, *The Arabian Nights* (1885)

When I was a kid, my sister had a doll, a huge and life-like baby doll, which we christened "Big Bertha." She resembled a two-year-old child at a distance. In one of my infrequent but not insignificant episodes as a **scapegrace**, I decided to place Bertha outside in a sitting position right next to the busy road that passed our house. Scores of cars slowed down as the drivers thought they needed to avoid hitting a child—and perhaps thinking they should stop and help a poor little waif who was about to wander into traffic. They sped off as soon as they realized they'd been fooled by a simulacrum. A school bus passed by, but some of the

scapegraces inside were not fooled by Big Bertha—one of them spit on her from an open window.

My siblings thought all of this was hilarious, and even my mother tittered a bit before she made me bring Bertha back inside, so she wouldn't "cause an accident." To this day, decades later, the kinfolk still mention this incident when we get together. Meanwhile, Big Bertha, who we thought we'd stored away in a closet or the basement of my mother's house, is nowhere to be found. I like to imagine that she escaped one day and hitched a ride to somewhere she feels safe and better appreciated.

sciolist [SIGH-uh-list] (noun)

A person with a pretentious attitude of scholarship or superficial knowledge

"Mr. Westport, who was always peppering his conversation with polysyllabic malapropisms, looked mystified when Annabelle called him a **sciolist**."

sciuroid [sigh-OR-oid] (adjective)

Resembling or characteristic of a squirrel

"The nuts spilled onto the floor, and there was much **sciuroid** scurrying to scoop them up."

scobberlotcher [SKOB-er-LOT-cher] (noun)

An idle person

"We cannot tell which class was affected by your Mr. Beeston, but it is pretty clear that Aubrey himself was a **Scobberlotcher**."
—Charles Isaac Elton, *William Shakespeare, His Family and Friends* (1904)

I'm not a **scobberlotcher**, but I like the idea of having a few idle, serendipitous days. Something might happen. I might see something out of the ordinary. I might meet someone or go somewhere. I might stay up all night and sleep all day. I might have an adventure, or just hibernate. I might even stumble across something to write about. *Weeeee!*

scribacious [scrib-AY-shuss] (adjective)

Fond of writing

"Heraud is a loquacious **scribacious** little man, of middle age, of parboiled greasy aspect, whom Leigh Hunt describes as 'wavering in the most astonishing manner between being Something and Nothing.'"
—Thomas Carlyle, *The Correspondence of Thomas Carlyle and Ralph Waldo Emerson* (1899)

I don't know any **scribacious** people. It is incomprehensible to me that anyone would waste their time scribbling for the unappreciative masses, the aimless, anonymous websurfers trolling for "nude girls dancing on airplane wings" (an actual Google search that, inexplicably, brought someone to my blog) and other such sordid topics, unless said scrivener was being highly compensated. "Only a fool writes for anything other than money," said Dr. Johnson. Writing for the sake of writing? I can't imagine such an affliction. No, I can't conceive of anyone needing such a useless outlet for their interior ruminations. Can you?

scripturient [scrip-TOOR-ee-uhnt] (adjective)

Having a violent desire to write

"And as for the 'lady novelist,' who supplies the circulating libraries with endless small reading, one feels that she is a curious product of this **scripturient** age. No doubt she fills some useful, or necessary, purpose in the subtle economy of this mysterious universe; but what it is, besides making a little money for herself, and providing a stimulus to the trades of paper-making, printer, and binding, one must wait to know until the 'great day' when all secrets will be revealed."
—G. W. Foote, "The Mighty Atom," in *Freethinker* (1896)

My, how sexist. It should be noted, however, that Foote was comparing the "lady novelists" of his own day to Charlotte Brontë ("a Titaness" he called her) and (Ms.) George Elliot ("full of intellect and power"), whom he called "mighty predecessors."

I can't say I've ever experienced **scripturience**—though I think you could say I have a strong urge to write, bordering on obsession. But violence? Let's say you were some kind of busybody censor who somehow inserted yourself into my circle of acquaintance. Would I hit you over the head with my thesaurus if you tried to prevent me from pounding the keys? Maybe, if you were insistent and persistent about it. And it might not be such a terrible thing. It would give me something exciting to write about.

scuppernong [SKUP-er-nong] (noun)

A type of grape, usually green or bronze in color, or a wine made from this grape

"I must here relate a fact, at the danger of appearing vain to some, viz.: I was written to, from the lower part of our state, to come down (about eighty miles), and instruct how to make the highly reputed, best **Scuppernong** wines, and was offered $4 a day from starting to returning." —Sidney Weller, "Vineyards at the South," in *The Industrial Resources, etc., of the Southern and Western States* (1853)

I first encountered this word when I read *To Kill a Mockingbird* a long time ago. Whenever I hear that title, I think of the film and Gregory Peck, a great actor and orator. I never get tired of hearing his voice. He could say a silly word like "**scuppernong**" with the kind of resonant enunciation that would make you want to go out and buy a bunch of grapes.

sedulous [SEJ-uh-luss] (adjective)

Diligent; painstaking; industrious

"All of his **sedulous** efforts came to naught when a meteorite crashed through the roof."

selcouth [SELL-kooth] (adjective)

Something rare or wonderful

"This guide...without either rhyme or reason, or any apparent cause, he bursts out with Stentorian voice into a most **selcouth** roar of song!"

—James Baillie Fraser, *Travels in Koordistan, Mesopotamia, &c.* (1840)

I used to go to sleep to the roar of surf. It was a recording of waves breaking on a beach, and the soothing, repetitive swooshing drowned out some annoying ambient sounds, allowing me to drift off to the **selcouth** Isle of Morpheus.

sermocination [sur-MO-cin-AY-shun] (noun)

The making of speeches or sermons; sermonizing

"Ephraim's park-bench **sermocination** drove away everyone except the squirrels."

shemozzle [shuh-MOZ-ul] (noun)

A state of confusion and chaos; an uproar

"'What a **shemozzle**, isn't it?' he said dazedly. 'I think we'd better get out of this don't you?'"
—Roland Pertwee, *Men of Affairs* (1922)

A few years ago, when I lived in a slightly more urban area, one of my Saturday night entertainments was simply to look out of my living-room window at a noisy **shemozzle**. A crowd of drunken young men would often spill out of a divey bar across the street that called itself The Oasis (but that I called The Fight Club). Inevitably, violent spats would break out, including knife-wielding contretemps. The fracas would eventually draw a wailing squad car to the scene, at which point all the dipsomaniacs and belligerents would scatter, roach-like, in all directions. It was better than reality TV.

shrift [shrift] (noun)

Confession (implying penance and absolution)

"*Benvolio:* See, where he comes. So please you step aside,
I'll know his grievance, or be much denied.

Montague: I would thou wert so happy by thy stay
To hear true **shrift**. Come, madam, let's away"
—William Shakespeare, *Romeo and Juliet,* Act I, Scene 1 (1597)

"*Ratcliffe:* Make a short **shrift**; he longs to see your head."
—William Shakespeare, *Richard III,* Act III, Scene 4 (1597)

I think this word is only used today in the phrase "short **shrift**," which originated with Shakespeare (at least his is the first recorded use of it) and has come to mean brushing off someone else's feelings in an offhand, callous manner, not a confession. I suppose you could call a genuine confession a long **shrift**. But your priest might disapprove.

simoleon [suh-MO-lee-un] (noun)

One dollar

"'T'ought I was lyin' about the money, did ye? Well, you can frisk me if you wanter. Dat's the last **simoleon** in the treasury. Who's goin' to pay?' The cattleman's clear grey eyes looked steadily from under his grizzly brows into the huckleberry optics of this guest. After a little he said simply, and not ungraciously, 'I'll be much obliged to you, son, if you won't mention money any more.'"
—O. Henry, "Hygeia at the Solito" in *Heart of the West* (1907)

I have one of those golden **simoleon** coins, and I don't know what to do with it. Somehow, I don't think most cashiers or bus drivers would appreciate being paid with a one-dollar coin. And it's too pulchritudinous to spend casually. George Washington appears a bit more contemporary on it than he does on the quarter, with an expression of what looks like mild disgust, as if about to pontificate on the contemporary political milieu—though it may just be because of his ill-fitting teeth.

sitooterie [sit-OOT-er-ee] (noun)

A gazebo; an outdoor structure to "sit out" in

"On sunny days, Angus and Fenella did their spooning in the **sitooterie**."

sitzfleisch [SITS-flysh] (noun)

The ability to endure or persist through determination

"Two years before, while Leila was still at school, he had begun his great task, and though often he had left it untouched for a few months (for the worthy doctor, it must be confessed, possessed but little of what the Germans call **Sitzfleisch**), he had but lately brought it to a close."
—Lise Boehm, "His First Review," in *Belgavia* (1888)

I'm all about **sitzfleisch**, come to think of it. In my life I've seen someone close to me succumb to alcoholism, lived in a rural area and then moved to New York City, overcome painful shyness (though I backslide), been fired, been rejected by friends both male and female, been depressed, failed in business, had to reinvent myself, blah, blah, blah, *boo, hoo, hoo.* It's not anything out of the ordinary, but ordinary in this world can be awful. But not, for me at least, unbearable. **Sitzfleisch** hasn't gotten me "far," but it's gotten me somewhere.

skyey [SKY-ee] (adjective)

Of or from the skies; resembling the skies; lofty

"She built **skyey** castles in her mind, even as her sneakers trod the linoleum."

slitheroo [slith-er-OO] (verb)

To slowly slide with a gliding motion

"Don't **slitheroo** thet way, Harve. Short's the trick, because no sea's ever dead still...."
—Rudyard Kipling, *Captains Courageous* (1897)

I didn't know there was a word for it until recently, but now I know that I **slitheroo** every morning as I descend to the commuter train platform at the station, sliding and gliding (and squeezing) past the commuters who insist on standing still on the escalator. I have no patience for riding escalators without also walking down or up the steps, even when I don't have a train to catch. Passive ascending and descending? That's for elevators.

"**Slitheroo**" makes me think of snakes, too. I knew a guy in college who kept a snake in a bag in his dorm-room closet. At least he said he did. I never had a desire to see it, and he never offered to show it to me. Now I wonder if he was putting me on.

slubberdegullion [SLUB-er-dee-GULL-yun] (noun)

A mean, filthy wretch; a slobberer

"Derwin feared he would have to pay for the mad revels of the night, and indeed he awoke that morning in a knot of sodden sheets, feeling like a **slubberdegullion**."

snollygoster [SNOL-ee-gost-er] (noun)

A shrewd, unprincipled person

"When the 'customer service representative' asked for his password, Herbert realized he was dealing with a **snollygoster**."

solivagant [so-LIV-uh-gunt] (noun or adjective)

Wandering alone

"Dick walks out to view the created cosmos, and plays the **solivagant** for about ten years—an undaunted ugly duckling of a fellow!"
—G. F. Monkshood, *Rudyard Kipling: An Attempt at Appreciation* (1899)

Solivagant is how I roll at times. One day I was walking across Manhattan, from my dentist's (alright, *endodontist's*) office on Madison Avenue to the train station on the West Side—or at least I thought I was. As usual, I was more in my head than on the street, and somehow I ended up on the decidedly eastern Third Avenue. I tend to overdose on reverie while walking alone, perhaps more so than ever when half my face is numb after a root canal.

somniculous [som-NIC-yoo-luss] (adjective)

Sleepy or drowsy

"She soon went to sleep, but dreamt of distresses and vexations, of exertions demanded, and powers not to be excited; of falling from precipices, of painful adieus, and of boats foundering in shoreless waters, and was haunted by all the train of **somniculous** misery, which the superstitious resolve into causes, and the less weak into effects."
—Laetitia Matilda Hawkins, *The Countess and Gertrude* (1812)

I sometimes get that falling feeling when I'm about to go to sleep. (I suppose that's where the phrase "falling asleep" comes from.) I'm sure it has to do with some **somniculous** lizard part of my brain suddenly realizing that my body is horizontal instead of vertical.

spanghew [SPANG-hyoo] (verb)

To throw or jerk violently, to cause to fly into the air, to jump like a toad or frog

"Damien enjoyed sneaking up behind Mildred, tapping her on the shoulder, and watching her **spanghew**."

spondulicks [spon-DOO-lix] (noun)

Money; cash

"I haven't got enough **spondulicks** to take a street-car ride."
—Alice Hegan Rice, *Calvary Alley* (1918)

Why do I still pay for almost every minor purchase with **spondulicks**, when almost every emporium I visit has a card swiper at the register? I do have a debit card. I just don't use it much. I think I like the physicality of the transaction, feeling those grubby pieces of paper and oily coins in my hands. Anything that can bring me down to earth from the digital Arcadia I dwell in for most of the day is salubrious.

spoony [SPOO-nee] (adjective)

Foolish, silly, ridiculously sentimental, lovesick

"I even walk, on two or three occasions, in a sickly, **spoony** manner, round and round the house after the family are gone to bed, wondering which is the eldest Miss Larkins's chamber."
—Charles Dickens, *David Copperfield* (1850)

I often find myself walking around the house late at night, too, with the lights off, carrying a flashlight, making sure the doors are locked. It's loony but not **spoony**.

squintifego [squin-teh-FAY-go] (adjective or noun)

Squinting; one who squints

"Having lost his glasses in the fight, Clive stumbled home **squintifego**, bumping into light posts, parked cars, and trash cans, as if in a drunken stupor. As he reached his door, he stepped on the cat, which let out a piercing cry that could be heard all over the neighborhood."

I even squint while wearing my glasses, as if it will somehow make the words I read on screen all day (I'm an editor) make more sense than they do. I used to squint when I wore contact lenses, too, but that was because it made them focus better.

Evil doers on TV and in films tend to squint while hatching their diabolical plans. And people assume you're thinking cynical thoughts when you look at them **squintifego**—as if squinting somehow gives one the ability to "see through" facades and deceptions. Next time someone says something unpleasant to you, try cocking your head a little and squinting at them. Chances are, the better angels of their nature will take over, they'll sputter a bit, and then recant.

Or maybe they'll just ask you if you forgot your glasses.

sternutation [ster-nyuh-TAY-shun] (noun)

The act or sound of sneezing

"Tabby, the omnipresent housecat, seemed to delight in Humphrey's constant **sternutation**."

I rarely sneeze, but people around me seem to do it often. I'm tired of blessing them—how did that custom get started anyway? Who am I to confer blessings on **sternutation**?

stultiloquence [stul-TILL-o-kwinse] (noun)

Foolish talk, idiotic discourse, or babble

"....but Saul, seldom sent to school, seldom said a single shrewd saying, and seldom showed signs of striving to say: so some said he seemed a somnolent sap-head, surpassingly sufflated with stupid **stultiloquence**."
—Francis Channing Woodworth, "Story of Saul Simpleton" (1852)

Overheard on the bus one evening: "There were too many yuppies. I need some rhythm in my life. Not just frolicking. That's just me being hickey, I guess...."

This was a rather parvenu-sounding woman burbling into her phone in the seat behind me. I couldn't help puzzling over what this little **stultiloquent** discourse meant. Do yuppies still exist? What does "hickey" mean? I suppose there are still young, urban professionals swimming around, even in the current economic malaise, but they no longer constitute a distinct social movement, I don't believe. As for "hickey," if she wasn't referring to herself as a passionate welt, she must have meant "hickish"—i.e., unsophisticated. "Hickey" people must prefer rhythm to frolicking, repetition to playfulness.

Personally, I prefer my frolicking to be rhythmic.

sublittoral [sub-LIT-er-uhl] (adjective)

Several related meanings: "Of or relating to the deeper part of a lake below the area in which rooted plants grow." "Permanently covered with sea water." "Under the shore." Used figuratively, it seems to mean "underwater" or "muffled."

"On the other hand, as long as the bed of the sea remained stationary, THICK deposits cannot have been accumulated in the shallow parts, which

are the most favourable to life....These remarks apply chiefly to littoral and **sublittoral** deposits."
—Charles Darwin, *The Origin of Species* (1859)

I haven't taken a bath in years. No, it's not a lack of hygiene; it's that I'm a shower man. To me, a bath seems like a luxury, a waste of time and water. "Drawing" the bath, lowering myself in, feeling around for the soap or sponge like a scavenging fish after some smaller sea creature, then washing myself in slow motion, as one tends to do **sublittoral**—it all seems very leisurely and Victorian. Then, too, I don't know how to wash my hair in the bathtub. But my main problem is that it feels delightful. It's like a trip back to the womb, and I'm tempted to linger and savor it—not good if I have to be somewhere in an hour.

sudoriferous [soo-duh-RIF-er-us] (adjective)

Producing or secreting sweat

"'It is absurd to expect a man of my capabilities to engage in **sudoriferous** efforts,' declared Dr. Smith as the Major handed him a shovel. He considered any physical labor beneath him, much to the annoyance of the shipwrecked crew."

suilline [SOO-il-line] (adjective)

Of or relating to pigs

"Little Freida's **suilline** appetite surprised everyone at the table."

surquedry [SUR-qued-ree] (noun)

Pride, arrogance, presumption or insolence

"Thou unprofitable spinster! Did I not bid thee mind the wax there by the hearth, lest it grew too hot? And see! It runneth about the ashes, and much good shall it serve for making of candles! I do wonder at thy light thoughts and over-much **surquedry**! There is no good husbandry in thee! A pretty piece of goods to find a mate for!"

—Edward Gilliat, *Forest Outlaws* (1887)

Surquedry is something I can't abide in a person. And when arrogance and stupidity are combined in a single character, the person is inevitably, in my experience, a walking disaster, creating chaos in whatever situation they encounter. I've dealt with arrogant people, and it's tolerable, as long as they are also smart. You just have to humor them, and they'll let you be. I've known stupid people too, and they're also manageable, because they're easy to manipulate. But an arrogant *and* stupid person? Run! Run away as fast as you can. Especially if they are also charming in some way. We've had presidents like that, not so long ago, and look where that's taken us.

But you'll find these people while walking down the street, too—like the guy in the Cadillac SUV who almost ran me over the other day, even though I had the pedestrian right of way. I almost got his license-plate number. Yes, SUV: **Surquedry** Ultimate Vanity.

susurrous [soo-SIR-uss] (noun)

A sound like rustling or whispering

"Though John was dismayed when his experimental film was projected upside down, the **susurrous** audience was clearly intrigued."

"Gentle winds had lulled the swell and the continual **susurrus** of the south wind enticed them towards the deep."
—Virgil, *The Aeneid* (19 BC?)

I like "white noise" and similar soundscapes, and the **susurrus** of a recording of ocean waves, as I wrote above, often entices me towards the deep—deep sleep, that is.

syllabub [SILL-uh-bub] (noun) (Also spelled sillabub)

A drink or, with gelatin added, a dessert, consisting of wine or liquor mixed with sweetened milk or cream

"Hey, Bub, I'll have some more of that delicious **syllabub** if you wouldn't mind passin' it over this way. No, I mean the **syllabub**. *Syllabub*! Don't you know English?"

sylvestral [SILL-vess-truhl] (adjective)

Pertaining to trees

"Xavier, lost in a thicket, was nevertheless awed by the **sylvestral** beauty of the canopy overhead."

T

talion [TAL-ee-un] (noun)

Punishment that fits the crime, as in "an eye for an eye"

"The first question, then, is what is the suitable method of instituting a process on behalf of the faith against witches. In answer to this it must be said that there are three methods allowed by Canon Law. The first is when someone accuses a person before a judge of the crime of heresy, or of protecting heretics, offering to prove it, and to submit himself to the penalty of **talion** if he fails to prove it. The second method is when someone denounces a person, but does not offer to prove it and is not willing to embroil himself in the matter...."
—Heinrich Kramer and James Sprenger, *Malleus Maleficarum* (1487)

Heretics and witches. I guess I am the former (by the standards of the time when *Malleus Maleficarum* was written), and I know someone who calls herself the latter. "Are you a good witch or a bad witch?" It's not always that simple. The witch I know is one of those crazy cat ladies and is pretty benign, though—except when she makes someone spontaneously combust. I wonder what the **talion** would be for that.

tantara [TAN-tah-rah] (noun)

A trumpet or horn fanfare

"Augusta always made quite an impression. Whenever she entered a room, I could almost hear a **tantara**."

tarradiddle [tar-uh-DID-el] (noun)

A small lie, or a bit of nonsense

"What is conjuring, when you come to think of it, but simply one big **tarradiddle**—a fib in action, so to speak, from beginning to end?"

—Angelo John Lewis, *Conjurer Dick, or the Adventures of a Young Wizard* (1885)

The adventures of a young wizard—now there's a great theme for a book, or even a series of books. Or a movie. No **tarradiddle**! Someone should take that idea and run with it.

tatterdemalion [tat-er-de-MAYL-yun] (noun)

A person who dresses in rags; a ragamuffin

"Despite his sizable fortune, Cedric insisted on dressing like a scarecrow. Though he was often mistaken for a vagrant, he told anyone who cared to inquire that he was 'a mere **tatterdemalion**.'"

tergiversate [TER-jih-ver-sayt] (verb)

To be evasive or ambiguous; equivocate; shilly shally

"But unfortunately the expulsion of James II, which he called his 'abdication,' compelled him to use all reserve, to shuffle and to **tergiversate**, in order to avoid making William out a usurper."
—Jean-Jacques Rousseau, *The Social Contract* (1893)

I'm not a "foodie." When confronted by a menu in a restaurant, my tendency is to **tergiversate** until the waiter starts hovering, and then order the chicken. I'd prefer that someone order for me, though I sometimes end up regretting it. When I was in Morocco on a business trip years ago, someone did order for me. And I ended up eating pigeon and rice. With my hands, in the Moroccan fashion. And it tasted just like... chicken.

testudinate [teh-STOOD-in-it] (adjective or noun)

Of or pertaining to a turtle or tortoise

"I looked out of the bedroom window at the furious blizzard and felt a **testudinate** desire to pull the covers over my head."

tittup [TIT-up] (noun or verb)

A caper or prance; to move in a lively way

"'Well,' he says, 'it's not much of a place for a **tittup**. There are one or two jolly old cockalorums there, and, when the season's on, you can go on the scoop in the way of a music-caper, or a hop, and you can get rid of the stuff there as well as anywhere.'"
—Francis Cowley Burnand, *More Happy Thoughts* (1871)

I haven't felt much in the mood to **tittup** lately. Scramble the letters and you get "putt it." That's more like it.

tittynope [TIT-ee-nohp] (noun)

A small quantity of something left over

"Jebediah kept the late Captain Wagstaff's wooden leg in the attic, as a memento of his days at sea with the old salt. But after the cursed termites got to it, only a **tittynope** remained."

I don't know why I have a hard time throwing leftovers away. We sometimes order Chinese, and there's always a **tittynope** of lo mein still in the refrigerator the next day, slowly congealing. Most unappetizing. I don't think any amount of microwaving can resurrect such remains into an edible state. "Lo mein" is Chinese for "tossed noodles," by the way. And that's what I should do—toss it.

tohubohu [TOE-hoo-BO-hoo] (noun)

Chaos, confusion

"....it is now easy to see that this bird is the Creator walking in chaos, brooding over the primitive mish-mash or **tohu-bohu**, and finally hatching the egg of the world."
—Viktor Rydberg, Rasmus Björn Anderson, James William Buel, *Teutonic Mythology* (1907)

The technological world that surrounds us today is "an integral of the **tohubohu**," according to literary critic Thomas M. Kavanagh in his book *The Limits of Theory*. It is no longer possible, he writes, to find anywhere on earth that is not flooded with what he calls "the diluvian waters of our racket."Depends on what you consider racket, I guess. I'd say there are limits to this theory.

This is what happens when you stop to shop at Stop N Shop, the local supermarket, at 11 PM. You give the checkout lassie a Jackson and a penny to pay for your $19.91 purchase of a few comestibles. She hands you a $10 bill in change, while giggling and conversing with the bag wrangler at the other end of the conveyer belt, who is stuffing your milk, Grape Nuts, yogurt, and mini-bagels into your reusable grocery tote.

There arrives a moment of total **tohubohu**. "Didn't I just hand her a twenty?" you think. "Um, wait," you say. "Is my change ten dollars—or ten cents?"

At this, the giggling ceases, and she finds it necessary to grab your receipt out of the tote. She studies it for a second, then exclaims "Oh, thank you, thank you!" and snatches back the Hamilton, replacing it in your palm with a dime. An "I'm SO sorry" and more "thank yous" are received, along with more giggling.

Apparently, pointing out her mistake is humorous, but is nevertheless a conscientious act worthy of Honest Abe. And I have met the **tohubohu**.

tourbillon [toor-bee-YON] (noun)

A whirlwind or vortex

"In this state of things, had I accepted and returned home, do you think that a seat upon the bench would have removed me from the **tourbillon** of politics?"
—John Quincy Adams, letter (1811)

These days, in English, a **Tourbillon** most often refers to a fancy type of watch. My own watch is nothing so elegant: it's an L.L. Bean field watch. When the battery went dead recently, and I didn't have time to replace it for a week, I took it off and felt naked for a few days—as well as in a **tourbillon** of confusion about what time it was.

triskaidekaphobia [tris-kye-dek-uh-FOE-bee-uh] (noun)

Fear of the number 13

"It was Friday the 13th, but nothing unlucky had happened. Ethan found this confusing and almost disappointing, since he always deferred to his **triskaidekaphobia**."

I was in a building in Manhattan one day, a very tony Upper East Side apartment building (where I accompanied someone on a doctor visit), complete with uniformed doormen, mahogany-paneled elevators, and art-deco chandeliers. No 13th floor, however. It's surprising to me (but maybe it shouldn't be) that the sort of person (pecunious) who can afford to live in such a domicile would suffer from **triskaidekaphobia**—or if they do, would be puerile enough not to realize that the 14th floor is actually....

truckle [TRUK-ul] (verb)

To yield or bend obsequiously to another's will; to submit, give in; to creep

"'You must never **truckle** to the Colonel's whims, Miranda,' Mrs. Chuzzlewit warned, 'or you will end up crushed beneath the grinding heel of his boot.' She paused, searching for the proper simile. 'Like one of his malodorous cigar butts.'"

truttaceus [troo-TAY-shuss] (adjective)

Pertaining to or like a trout

"....crowded with the boats of paradise, we would fancy parades and serenades mid its roral gales, lepid glens and **truttaceus** charms...."
—Anonymous, in *The New Rugbeian* (1859)

A "chub" and a catfish—those are the only types of fish I ever caught. They were hardly **truttaceus**, and I threw them back. That's the kind of guy I am. ("Roral," by the way, means "dewy.")

tufthunter [TUFT-hunt-er] (noun)

A sycophant or toady

"Mr. Brandon was a **tufthunter** of the genteel sort; his pride being quite as slavish, and his haughtiness as mean and cringing, in fact, as poor Mrs. Gann's stupid wonder and respect for all the persons whose names are written with titles before them."
—William Makepeace Thackeray, *A Shabby Genteel Story* (1840)

One of my professors in college—who was also a famous novelist—was highly susceptible to **tufthunters**. It was interesting to watch someone so esteemed and seemingly brilliant be manipulated by the flattery of mere students. Interesting and, well, nauseating.

tushery [TUHSH-er-ee] (noun)

The use of affectedly archaic language

"Ay, friend, a whole tale of **tushery**. And every tusher tushes me so free, that may I be tushed if the whole thing is worth tush."
—Robert Louis Stevenson, in a letter to his editor, W. E. Henley (1883)

We have to wonder how this word (which Stevenson coined and which became popular enough, at least for a while, to be included in dictionaries) relates to "tush," a word that refers to "the hinder," as we kids used to say. Where did the word come from? Not "your butt," as a young relative of mine would suggest. More likely, it derives from the interjection "tush," more a sound than a word, which is used to signal disapproval, as in "That book is *tush*."

I find **tushery** rather amusing. Using archaic words, in a context that gives the listener at least some inkling of what you're blathering about, can trick people into thinking you're more educated that you are. So memorize some Shakespeare quotations from brainyquote.com and impress your friends and enemies with your ~~tushery~~ erudition. Of course, not everything Shakespeare said sounds archaic today. To wit:

"A fool thinks himself to be wise, but a wise man knows himself to be a fool."

twee [twee] (adjective)

Nauseatingly sweet or cute

"Herb was always searching for birthday cards that weren't insulting, insipid or **twee**. 'No easy task,' he said."

U

ubiety [yoo-BYE-ih-tee] (noun)

The state of being in a particular place

"Hell is a definite locality, as all finite beings must be confined to a place, as the wicked are not in heaven, and as hell and heaven constitute the only two places. They cannot be everywhere, because they are not infinite. **Ubiety** belongs necessarily to finite beings. Therefore the condemned must be in a place."
—Johann Gerhard, quoted in *That Unknown Country* (1888)

My **ubiety** involves being at 40.748 latitude and -74.050 longitude. I can't say I'm rejoicing in my idyll here, but there are worse places.

ugsome [UG-sum] (adjective)

Horrible, loathsome

"Since she has lain into your arms,
She shall not lye in mine;
Since she has kiss'd your **ugsome** mouth,
She never shall kiss mine."
—Sir Walter Scott, "Sir Hugh Le Blond" (1802)

I live in a place where it snows in the winter. After a blizzard, when the snow begins to melt at last in our urban neighborhood, it can be pretty **ugsome**. As the frozen mounds (often not very white anymore) dissolve into puddles, they reveal flotsam and jetsam that's been buried since before the snowpocalypse: a denuded Christmas tree, a dead computer monitor, a broken clock, a forsaken doll, and a huge variety of twisted wrappers, soiled containers, and even canine excrement. As a frequent pedestrian within the urban snow-pack, which would I rather have: a frigid, pristine world of difficult mobility or a more temperate realm of **ugsome** filth but free-ranging locomotion? The latter, but I don't have to like it.

ultracrepidarian [ul-tra-krep-ih-DARE-ee-an] (noun or adjective)

Someone who expresses an opinion or offers advice about a subject they know nothing about

"'The labor? It was a breeze! Right, Honey?' said new dad Matt. '**Ultracrepidarian**!' new mom Sandra replied. 'Told ya,' Matt added."

usufruct [YOO-zoo-fruct] (noun)

The right to use and enjoy something belonging to someone else without it being destroyed or injured

"'Do you mind if I have **usufruct** with your jacket?' Winnie asked. 'Yes I mind!' said Jane. 'For heaven's sake. I just had it dry-cleaned.'"

uxorious [uk-SAR-ee-us] (adjective)

Excessively dependent on, attached to, or doting on one's wife

"The queen asked her false husband whether it were possible to make her parrot talk, and he, in a moment of **uxorious** weakness, promised to make it speak. He laid his body aside, and sent his soul into the parrot. Immediately, the true king jumped out of his Brahmin body and resumed that which was legitimately his own, and then proceeded, with the queen, to wring the neck of the parrot."
—Sabine Baring Gould, *The Book of Were-Wolves* (1865)

Uxorious? I am married; let's not go there.

V

valgus [VAL-guss] (noun or adjective)

Bone deformity; the state of being bowlegged or knock-kneed

"'Oh, I see you have **valgus**,' Dr. Sapirstein said.
'Huh?' said Billy-Bob.
'Your legs.'
'What about 'em?'
'They're, uh, perfect for riding your horse I guess, hmm?'
'Well...yup. I reckon they are good for that. But it doesn't matter now. I lost my job on the ranch, dag burnit.'
'Really? Why?'
'I couldn't keep my calves together.'"
—an old joke

My **valgus** is in my left little finger, which I broke in gym class in junior high school. The school nurse thought it was sprained, but it was broken, and I never got it set. When it healed, it was a little crooked. It still is. It's my one imperfection (other than a weakness for puns).

vecordious [veh-KOR-dee-us] (adjective)

Mad, crazy, senseless

"Last weekend, when I went to visit my **vecordious** Aunt Helen at the Mayfield Psychiatric Hospital, I encountered an escaped mental patient in the parking lot. She was wearing a dress that appeared to be stitched together from latex gloves and a plastic bucket on her head as she crawled toward me like some kind of human tarantula."

Much could be said about the **vecordious** Congressional machinations often displayed in Washington, D.C., but I prefer to comment on events closer to home.

I was in a fast-food restaurant the other day (yes, I do patronize such places at times, especially if in a hurry) when an elderly, **vecordious** lady walked in and started yelling at another woman, who was sitting, alone, at a table enjoying her lunch. They seemed to know each other. The crazy lady wasn't angry; she was just talking much too loudly for a public place. And she was full of advice, telling the other woman to be sure to bring her own toilet paper when using a public restroom, to do background checks on her neighbors, to always be sure to carry enough money for bus fare, and so on.

The other woman replied minimally, in a soft voice, I suppose to encourage her crazy acquaintance to pipe down, and tried to continue eating her lunch. The whole restaurant was staring. But the harangue continued, until the other woman got up and hurried out of the restaurant. I felt sorry for her, and worried that the crazy lady would turn to me next. But instead she went into the restroom and stayed there until someone started banging on the door. "I'll be out in a minute!" she screamed, adding that everyone should bring their own toilet paper. She didn't sound angry, just LOUD. And **vecordious**.

velleity [vuh-LEE-ih-tee] (noun)

A slight wish; a mild desire

"Again the idea came to him to give up his task and go away, but this **velleity** only lasted a second: it was now too late to draw back."
—Fyodor Dostoyevsky, *Crime and Punishment* (1866)

I have many **velleities** throughout the day, like anyone: to be warmer or cooler, for a cup of coffee, to conjure something to write about, to retrocede time. For a break. For a laugh. For things that might surprise you. Sometimes they even come true.

verbigeration [ver-bij-uh-RAY-shun] (noun)

Compulsive repetition of meaningless or stereotyped words and phrases

"A patient who developed the stereotyped antic of keeping her toes in constant movement while in bed, had the following **verbigeration**: 'I can't keep on twiddling my toes like this for ever, I can't keep on twiddling my toes like this for ever, I can't keep on...' etc., etc."

—William Henry Butter Stoddart, *Mind and Its Disorders* (1908)

When extreme, **verbigeration** is a sign of mental illness. But it's fairly common, and vexatious, in my experience. I know persons, who shall be nameless, who persistently repeat the following:

"Pretty much"
"And your point is?"
"The good news is..."
"What's interesting is..."
"Okay...okay...okay..."
"Oh my God..."
"No problem"

I don't think I'm implicated in this habitual verbal prattle, but I do repeat certain phrases internally as I go about my quotidian doings. I won't list them here, for fear they will lose their efficacy. These are just mental placeholders, little catchphrases that blot out disturbing or pestiferous cogitations. Sort of like "every good boy does fine," though they're a lot quirkier than that.

vicambulation [vye-cam-byoo-LAY-shun] (verb)

To walk about in the streets

"Then he took to **vicambulation**, and lo! over the most magnificent shop in Riverdale—a shop brilliant with gold and silver plate, and blazing with superb gems—he perceived the name of Boss."
—Mortimer Collins, *The Vivian Romance* (1870)

The pleasing distinction about living in a dense metropolis is that one can walk to find just about any necessity. And I do. I also **vicambulate**, more or less aimlessly, as a form of moving meditation.

vilipensive [vil-uh-PEN-siv] (adjective)

Abusive

"[T]ime was when even Rhedycina's learned bowers resounded to strains

not simply laudative of Oporto, but vituperative and **vilipensive** of Bourdeaux."
—Sir Morgan O'Doherty, "Remarks on Henderson the Historian," in *Blackwood's Edinburgh Magazine* (1824)

Try accusing someone of being "**vilipensive** of Bourdeaux" today. Make them scurry for the dictionary!

vinculation [vink-yoo-LAY-shun] (noun; verb form: **vinculate**)

The act of tying or binding

The elements of the continuity and permeability of the human spirit **vinculate** us with the elaborations of thought, the concatenation of ideas, the concepts and creations of the intelligences that have existed or that exist.
—Emilio J. Pasarell, "Ripples on the Surface of Great Themes," in *Inter-America* (1921)

I prefer loafers, just so I don't have to **vinculate** my shoelaces, which always seem to come untied, even when I double knot them. My brother-in-law avoids this problem—he never ties his shoes; he walks around with them untied. I don't think I could do that without tripping.

virga [VUR-guh] (noun)

Rain or snow that evaporates before it hits the ground

"Internal acacias thrive in the synaptic breeze off the conceptual sea, as mental clouds flee in formation, weeping curtains of **virga** from the sky."

This seems like a word that could also be used for half-baked notions or unfinished projects: **Virga**-like ideas for stories or artwork that seem fantastic when inspiration strikes but that then fade away when you don't get around to producing them—or that don't seem quite so fantastic the next morning.

volitant [VAHL-ih-tint] (adjective)

1. Flying, or capable of flying.
2. Moving about rapidly.

"When Mother gets violent, frying pans get **volitant**."

volitation [VAHL-ih-TAY-shun] (noun)

The act of flying; flight

"Dreams of **volitation** led Professor Spillings to invent many crash-prone flying machines."

wahala [wah-HAH-luh] (noun)

Trouble, hassle (noun; Nigerian pidgin English)

"Aaron had some dental **wahala** that he refused to ameliorate, much to the consternation of his brother Darren, who consulted for a dental-retainer manufacturer."

My hassle? The heavy-duty cord to my electric lawnmower—300 feet of kinked up, knotted up **wahala**. We have a tiny backyard that needs mowing about once a week. It's a simple enough task, except for the extension cord, which twists itself into a convoluted tangle of pure frustration. I keep unplugging myself because the cord won't stretch far enough with all its snags and snarls. Why can't someone genetically engineer grass to only grow to an inch and a half in length, anyway? We can put a man on the moon....

wallydrag [WAH-lee-drag] (noun)

Also: wallydraigle; a feeble or useless person; the youngest bird in the nest; the runt of the litter

"Deed, Miss Girzie, I feel for you. It's just like the cuckoo dabbing a **wallydraigle** out o' the nest; but I'll reason with her."
—John Galt, *The Last of the Lairds* (1826)

"Like an unstrung zither, I lie back, exhausted, useless, immobile and silent." That's a line that once came to me as I reclined on the couch after a busy day, when I was feeling like, yes, a **wallydrag**.

wamble [WHAM-bull] (verb)

To move in a wobbling or weaving manner; to rumble (as from an upset stomach)

"'Fancy her white hands getting redder every day, and her tongue losing its pretty up-country curl in talking, and her bounding walk becoming the regular Hintock shail and **wamble**!'

'She may shail, but she'll never **wamble**,' replied his wife, decisively."
—Thomas Hardy, *The Woodlanders* (1887) ("shail" means to walk sideways)

I have a (male) neighbor who wears a wig and a dress—a miniskirt, in fact—and **wambles** down the street in high heels. But I haven't seen him lately. Or maybe I have, and I just didn't recognize him out of drag. To each his/her own.

wazzock [WAZ-uk] (noun)

A nitwit; a stupid or annoying person

"'So a Forest Service worker started the immense wildfires in Colorado when she decided to burn a letter from her 'estranged husband' in the middle of a tinder-dry forest. Smart!' said Pete as he looked up from his newspaper. 'Couldn't this **wazzock** just tear up the jerk's letter at home and flush it down the toilet? It might have caused her sewer pipe to back up, but at least that would be a more manageable problem.'"

I haven't met a genuine **wazzock** (that I had to spend any significant time with) in ten years at least. Instead, I tend to have fleeting **wazzock** moments. For instance, I was once at an event where very hot coffee was being served in paper cups. I asked for "two cups," so I could put one cup inside the other to avoid burning my digits. The barista behind the counter poured me two cups of hot coffee before I could explain what I meant. Was he the **wazzock** or, uh, wazz I? It was the moment itself, I think.

Weltanschauung [VELT-an-shaowng] (noun; often capitalized)

A personal philosophy about life or the world; world view

"The **Weltanschauung**, the total world view, the apparent multiplicity of phenomena lost in the unity of eternal forces, this has been the goal of philosophic thinking."
—M. E. Haggerty, "Science and Democracy," in *Popular Science* (1915)

My **Weltanschauung**: We all have at least two sides—at least. There are hidden meanings in just about everything, often unconscious meanings. And our primary task is to reconcile opposites.

weltschmerz [VELT-shmayrts] (noun)

Sentimental pessimism

"The representatives of cosmic **Weltschmerz** are those poets whose first concern is not their personal fate, their own unhappiness...but who see first and foremost the sad fate of humanity and regard their own misfortunes merely as a part of the common destiny."
—Wilhelm Alfred Braun, *Types of Weltschmerz in German Poetry* (1905)

I don't mind realistic pessimism per se, but I find people who cherish their pessimism, who engage in **weltschmerz**, hard to take. They get angry when you try to make them feel better.

whigmaleerie [wig-muh-LEER-ee] (noun)

A notion or whim; also something contrived, a gimmick

"But, of course, if you'd be better suited with some French **whigmaleerie**, why, say so, and ha' done with it."
—Curtis Yorke, *The Other Sara* (1908)

Whigmaleeries can be dangerous. My wife and I were discussing possible Halloween costumes for a party we were invited to, and off the top of my head, I jokingly suggested she create a character named Helena Handbasket. I didn't expect her to take it seriously, but then she started constructing a basket to wear.

whilom [WY-lum] (adjective)

Former

"Natalia was astonished to see Bernardo, her **whilom** inamorato, perambulating down the street—the last person she wanted to see. She quickly hid behind a convenient pot of shrubbery."

widdendream [WID-in-dreem] (noun)

A state of confusion or mental disturbance

"Lucinda, already dizzy from the medication, experienced total
widdendream when the escalator suddenly changed direction."

Someone close to me, who shall be nameless, experienced **widdendream**
while under the influence, shall we say. This fellow imagined he was being
chased around the inside of an enormous cereal bowl by a gigantic spoon.
Some passersby apparently entered **widdendream** while trying to figure out
what his excited babbling was about.

"You don't hear about it anymore, but people are still visiting the cosmos."
—John Lennon

williwaw [WIL-ee-wa] (noun)

A sudden gust of wind or a violent commotion

"The parting of a staysail-sheet in a **williwaw**, when the sea was turbulent
and she was plunging into the storm, brought me forward to see instantly a
dark cliff ahead and breakers so close under the bows that I felt surely lost,
and in my thoughts cried, 'Is the hand of fate against me, after all, leading
me in the end to this dark spot?'"
—Joshua Slocum, *Sailing Alone Around the World* (1900)

I often feel that the "hand of fate is against me." Don't you? But sooner or
later (often much later), some **williwaw** comes along, and the perspective
changes, and I think, "That's the way it had to be, so *boo hoo hoo*...." Well, I
don't usually cry.

Sometimes I feel like I'm "sailing alone around the world," or nearly
so, too, but that's a different bottle of whine.

witenagemot [WIT-in-uh-guh-mot] (noun)

The assembly of the witan; the national council attended by the king, aldermen, bishops, and nobles

"The kingdom was ruled jointly by the king and the **witenagemot**, or meeting of the wise men, often expressed by the word *witan*, or the wise." —Cyril Ransome, *An Advanced History of England from the Earliest Times to the Present Day* (1899)

I'm mostly Anglo-Saxon (English) but also part Celtic (Welsh) and part a few other things. I'm interested in England's history, but ancestry doesn't mean much to me—I'm not interested in joining a **witenagemot**. But I love the English language and have devoted myself to it, for better or worse. For better *and* worse.

witticaster [WHIT-ih-kas-ter] (noun)

Someone who thinks they're funny—but they're not

"Olgar's speech is too rotten even for one who 'hath tippled somewhat already.' A post-prandial **witticaster** of our own day could not be nastier at the orgies of a party of bankers." —Edwin Sauter, *The Faithless Favorite* (1905)

Q: Why was the math book sad?
A: Because it had a lot of problems.

I love puns, and to me, they are very funny. They're also useful when you have to generate eye-catching headlines or little editorial tag lines quickly. But they are "the lowest form of humor" we're told (but poetry is much verse). Tell that to Shakespeare, who was full of puns, e.g., the cobbler who says he is a mender of men's soles in *Julius Caesar.*

What is the highest form of humor, anyway? Surely slapstick is the lowest form, not puns. You know, people slipping on banana peels.... Hmm, bananas. "Time flies like an arrow. Fruit flies like a...." No, I won't be a **witticaster**.

X

xanthochroi [ZANTH-a-croy] (noun)

Fair-skinned white people

"The **Xanthochroi** (fair whites) and the Melanochroi (dark whites) of Britain are, speaking broadly, distributed, at present, as they were in the time of Tacitus; and their representatives on the Continent of Europe have the same general distribution as at the earliest period of which we have any record."
—William Gregory Wood-Martin, *Traces of the Elder Faiths of Ireland: A Folklore Sketch* (1902)

I've always wondered why the "aliens" in science-fiction films and TV shows are most often portrayed as **xanthochroi** if they're not green. Real aliens, if you believe they exist and are visiting us, are said to be "greys." But Vulcans and Kryptonians and even E.T. are, it seems, white folks. I'm sure it has more to do with employment practices in Hollywood than with exobiology. Why do we accept that white actors, or even white puppets, can portray aliens but black actors would be unbelievable? Because we think of "aliens" as mirrors of ourselves, and we still live (here in the US) in a majority **xanthochroi** culture. That's my sociology lecture.

xanthodont [ZAN-thuh-dont] (noun)

A person with yellow teeth

"'The next patient is a **xanthodont**, doctor,' the hygienist said. 'What? I only treat humans!' the dentist exclaimed."

xeric [ZEER-ik] (adjective)

Referring to a dry environment

"'Oh, how **xeric**,' Mavis said, when her nephew, Trevor, showed her the pictures from Mars. 'Oh, they're not photocopies,' replied Trevor."

xilinous [ZIL-in-us] (adjective)

Of or pertaining to cotton

"'A **xilinous** swab is what I need!' Captain Morgan shouted. The first mate thought he was referring to a nefarious deck hand, but he only wanted to clean his ears."

xylology [zy-LAW-luh-jee] (noun)

The study of wood

"Dale was impressed by the lumber mill. 'I see you're a real expert in **xylology**,' he said after the tour. 'Nah, I just know a lot about wood,' said Pete."

Y

yaffle [YAF-ul] (noun)

A green woodpecker

"'What's that noise?' wondered Henry aloud, as the persistent tapping started up again. '**Yaffle**!' Katherine responded. 'It was a serious question,' said Henry. 'You don't need to call me names.'"

yapness [YAP-ness] (noun)

Hunger

"'Let's find a restaurant,' Sheila suggested. 'I'm feeling some **yapness**.' 'Why do we need a restaurant?' said Arnold. 'You can yap and yell at me right here.'"

yare [yair (yar)] (adjective)

Speedy, agile, nimble

"The juice of Egypt's grape shall moist this lip. **Yare**, **yare**, good Iras, quick—methinks I hear Antony call; I see him rouse himself /To praise my noble act; I hear him mock the luck of Caesar, which the gods give men /To excuse their after wrath."
—William Shakespeare, *Antony and Cleopatra*, Act V, Scene ii. (1623)

My escalator-riding technique is so *yare*.
   There are two types of people you encounter on an escalator: passive riders who stand still and ride up (or down) like plaster saints on a conveyor belt, and those who treat the escalator as a moving staircase to be climbed or descended actively. The latter requires sprightly zigging and zagging, not unlike the jogging of a running-back on a football field, to avoid the obstructionists, who will often stand two-abreast, blocking the forward momentum of the climber (me) as he attempts to catch his train or just

relieve his impatience with this odd form of travel. And it is odd, when you think about it—a moving staircase. People don't stand still on conventional stairs; why do they feel they can do so on these rolling steps? Be **yare** or be square, I say.

yegg [yeg] (noun)

A safecracker

"Arthur had forgotten the combination. 'We need a **yegg**,' he said with a sigh. 'Huh? Scrambled or over easy?' Mack snickered."

yonderly [YON-der-lee] (adjective)

Mentally or emotionally distant, morose, gloomy or aloof

"'I don't think I would be much fun today,' Anna said when she finally took Stan's call. 'I'm **yonderly**.' 'Where's that?' Stan asked."

Z

zaddik [ZOD-ihk] (noun)

A righteous and saintly person by Jewish religious standards

"He drew a beautiful picture of the ideal **zaddik**, who is 'so absorbed in meditation on the Divine wisdom that he cannot descend to the lower steps upon which ordinary people stand.'"
—Jacob Salmon Raisin, *The Haskalah Movement in Russia* (1914)

Hmm. I wonder if the meditation I do on the train each morning on my way to work will ever make a **zaddik** of me.

zarf [zarf] (noun)

A holder for a hot coffee cup

"The guest holds out the cup by the silver **zarf**, the attendant opening one hand places it under, then brings the palm of the other upon the top of the cup; the guest relinquishes his hold, and the attendant retires backward with the cup thus secured."
—David Urquhart, *The Spirit of the East* (1839)

Those little cardboard thingamabobs they put around your coffee cup at Starbucks are technically called "**zarfs**," although they will try to tell you they're called cup sleeves (how boring!). Whenever I forget my ceramic coffee mug at work, I have to use a paper cup, and they're too damn hot to hold—life is *tough*. There are no **zarfs** there, so I make my own, putting one (hot) paper cup inside another (cool) one. I'm resourceful! It does make it a bit harder to sip, though. Like I said, life is tough. (Wasn't there a cartoon alien named **Zarf**?)

zenzizenzizenzic [ZEN-zih-ZEN-zih-ZEN-zihk] (noun)

A number to the eighth power (the **zenzizenzizenzic** of 2 is 256)

"In their algebraic writings, and in some of the early English ones, the zenzic power is the square. From this and the word cube, various denominations of powers were formed, as zenzi-cubic for sixth, **zenzizenzizenzic** for eight, &c., from which we are now happily delivered."
—*The English Cyclopaedia* (1861)

I never liked math in school, which is why I became an English major, earning the pity, scorn, and opprobrium of all the "practical" people who didn't know a gerund from a quatrain. If you read about careers these days, a humanities degree is supposed to be economic suicide, a one-way ticket to life as a Walmart greeter. But somehow I've managed, against seemingly **zenzizenzizenzic**-like odds, to do alright, if not spectacularly, with my logophilia affliction. I don't know if anybody still majors in English, but I hope they do. Somebody has to maintain some standards, even at the risk of being labeled a "grammar Nazi," as I have been. I hate that. Call me a prose technician or a text engineer. Call me Ishmael....

zugzwang [TSOOG-tsvahng] (noun)

In chess, a position in which one player can move only with loss or severe disadvantage; metaphorically, a situation in which there are no good options

"White has struggled bravely and only loses by '**Zugzwang**'."
—*Lasker's Chess Magazine* (1905)

I haven't played chess in quite a while. I think I like the idea of chess, and the romantically medieval imagery of the pieces, more than the game itself, which I find protracted and full of **zugzwangs**, even if I'm winning. Too much like life. There have been times when I've felt like a pawn or a knight; never really like a king, a bishop, a rook, or a queen. And I rarely find that situations are black and white.

zymurgy [ZEI-mur-jee] (noun)

The study of fermentation

"'What's your major?' asked Jennifer. '**Zymurgy**!' Barry exclaimed before chugging the rest of the bottle."

169

ABOUT THE AUTHOR

Michael Gates is a logophile, a professional copy editor, and a compulsive blogger (at michaelgates.blogspot.com). He grew up in the wilds of upstate New York and now lives the high life in the Heights of Jersey City with his wife and son. He has written and published non-fiction and poetry, but most of his current literary efforts bend in the direction of short-short stories, also known as microfiction (mike-rofiction?). *The Word I'm Thinking Of* is his first book..